Clinical Confidentiality

Clinical Confidentiality

Charles Foster and Nicholas Peacock

6 Pump Court
Temple
London

This is a book about clinical confidentiality. It is not
a substitute for obtaining legal advice and no one
should rely on the information contained in it. The
authors and the publishers accept no liability in
relation thereto.

The text is up to date to 1 August 2000.

The authors assert their right to be identified as the
authors of this work under ss77 and 78 of the
Copyright, Designs and Patents Act 1988.

ISBN 1 871 241 51 0

Published by Monitor Press
Suffolk House
Church Field Road
Sudbury
Suffolk
CO10 2YA

Printed in Great Britain by
Short Run Press Ltd

About the authors

Charles Foster is a barrister practising from 6 Pump Court, Temple, London EC4, primarily in medical law. He read Law and Veterinary Medicine at St John's College, Cambridge, researched wild animal immobilization in Saudi Arabia, was a Research Fellow in the Department of Law at the Hebrew University, Jerusalem, research assistant to Aharon Barak, now President of the Supreme Court of Israel, and is a member of the Bars of England and the Republic of Ireland. He is the author of a number of publications, and a regular contributor to several legal and non-legal periodicals.

Nicholas A Peacock is a barrister practising from 6 Pump Court, Temple, London EC4, primarily in medical law. He read Law at Trinity Hall, Cambridge. He has contributed to several legal periodicals and lectures in medical law nationwide.

Preface

The law of confidentiality is an odd, chimeric animal. It has bits of equity, contract, tort and plain judicial frolic in it. And so it is hardly surprising that it lumbers a bit over rough ground.

Medical confidentiality cases have (generally) been argued before Queen's Bench judges (happy in commercial law) by medico-legal barristers (happy in tort) using Chancery cases (which relate to a dramatically different legal universe). And so it is hardly surprising that things are rather messy.

But it matters that the law gets it right. Medical secrets are important. Patients don't expect their doctors to chatter about them over beer and chips in the hospital canteen. If they did expect this, the patients would be coy about potentially relevant confidences. And that would be to the detriment of the patients and the doctors.

This book is written in an attempt to make the law useable. It puts in one place what it would otherwise take a lot of trips to obscure libraries to find out. And it tries to apply all the rarefied Chancery cases to practical clinical problems. If the book's emphasis is wrong, we hope it is insufficiently learned and too insultingly practical. There are other books which speculate interestingly on what the law might be. This book is as short as it could be without dangerous over-simplification.

Charles Foster and Nick Peacock,
Temple, EC4
August 2000

Contents

Preface. vii

Chapter 1:   Introduction: Why Bother to
             Keep Confidences? 1

Chapter 2:   The Common Law Obligation to
             Keep Confidences. 2

Chapter 3:   The Impact of Statute on the
             Law of Confidentiality. 23

Chapter 4:   Disclosure Where Litigation is
             Contemplated or Proceeding 29

Chapter 5:   The European Demension. 40

Chapter 6:   Rights of Access to Health Records
             Other Than in the Course of Litigation. 56

Chapter 7:   Remedies for Breach of Confidence 63

Chapter 8:   Precedents 71

Appendix 1: The General Medical Council's
             Guidelines on Confidentiality. 84

Appendix 2: The General Dental Council's
Guidelines on Confidentiality. 95

Appendix 3: The United Kingdom Central Council for
Nursing, Midwifery and Health Visiting
(UKCC) Guidelines on Confidentiality 97

Appendix 4: The Chartered Society of Physiotherapy's
Guidelines on Confidentiality 102

Appendix 5: The Royal College of Veterinary Surgeons'
Guidelines on confidentiality 107

Appendix 6: The Data Protection Act 1998 (Extracts) . . . 110

Appendix 7: Useful addresses 142

Index. 143

Chapter 1
Introduction: Why Bother to Keep Confidences?

1.1	There are two reasons why the courts think that doctors should keep confidences. These reasons are alluded to in most of the important judgments, but they are emphasised to widely differing degrees in those judgments.
1.2	The first reason is that, despite the absence of any general common law right to privacy, a limited, conditional right to confidentiality is a basic human right. Of course the courts have not usually expressed themselves this way, but this is always what they have meant. Being English, they have, until recently, felt happier to use the language of contract in saying why doctors should not chat incontinently about their patients' secrets: the language of implied obligations not to disclose secrets does less violence to judges' assumptions about the architecture of their legal world than does talk about fundamental rights and freedoms.
1.3	The second is that, if doctors are not forced to keep confidences, patients will feel inhibited about offering them. And that will be to everyone's disadvantage. A doctor needs to know potentially embarrassing secrets about patients in order to get diagnostic and therapeutic answers right. The patient needs the doctor to get the answers right.

Chapter 2
The Common Law Obligation to Keep Confidences

2.1	**The legal nature of the obligation**
2.1.1	Nobody really knows what the nature of the obligation is in England, and few care. The obligation to keep confidences is historically a bizarre cocktail of tort, equity, contract, property and downright judicial imagination.
2.1.2	In *Morrison v Moat* Turner VC said:

'Different grounds have indeed been assigned for the exercise of the jurisdiction ... but, upon whatever grounds the jurisdiction is founded, the authorities leave no doubt as to the exercise of it ...'[1]

In other words, arguing about the nature of the obligation is a waste of time: the obligation exists and has well recognised characteristics.

2.1.3	Of course one can have a pure contractual obligation to keep confidences. Where a relationship between a doctor and a patient is a contractual relationship, it would be neat pleading to allege an implied term as to confidentiality, but even there it is not necessary to do it. It is well established that a patient with whom a doctor has no contract is entitled to the same protection which an implied contractual obligation would give. Express contractual provision can of course do any-

---

1   (1851) 9 Hare 241, 255.

thing to obligations of confidentiality which statute will allow.

2.2   **The characteristics of the obligation: a summary**

2.2.1   (a) There is an important public interest in maintaining clinical confidentiality.

(b) That interest is so strong that the law imposes a duty on clinicians to maintain confidences.

(c) The duty to keep confidences is not absolute: sometimes the public interest in disclosure may override it.[2]

2.2.2   Thus clinicians must not disclose confidential information unless either:

(a) the public interest in disclosure outweighs the public interest in maintaining confidentiality; or

(b) statute/the disclosure process in litigation requires him to disclose it.

2.3   **Who can sue?**

2.3.1   The only person with locus standi to sue is the person to whom the duty of confidence is owed.[3]

2.3.2   Where the person whose confidence is at risk is dead, it is unlikely (by analogy with the parallel law of defamation) that proceedings restraining the publication of the information can be brought. But the position has not yet been decided in England, and the contrary view, based on the notion that it is unconscionable and therefore inequitable to divulge confidential information after the death of the person to whom the confidence is owed, is arguable.[4]

---

2   See *W v Egdell* [1990] 1 All ER 835, per Bingham LJ at 848.

3   *Fraser v Evans* [1969] 1 All ER 8. Note that where the Crown is owed a duty of confidence the Attorney General, representing the public interest, will be the appropriate claimant. Where confidential information has been passed by the original confider to another, intending that the assignee should enjoy the benefit of that information, the assignee may be able (per Lord Denning MR in *Fraser v Evans* at p361) to prevent disclosure of the information.

4   See Toulson RG, and Phipps, CM, *Confidentiality*, London: Sweet and Maxwell, 1996: 13-17.

2.4	**Who can be sued?**
2.4.1	The person who has breached the duty of confidentiality (obviously).
2.4.2	Less obviously, someone who has come into possession of the information and knows or suspects that it is confidential information but nonetheless publishes or intends to publish it.[5]
2.5	**What is confidential information?**
2.5.1	The best that the courts have been able to do is to produce the dizzyingly circular definition in *Saltman Engineering Co v Campbell Engineering Co Ltd*[6] which asserts that confidential information is information which has:

> '... the necessary quality of confidence about it, namely it must not be something which is public property and public knowledge ...'

2.5.2	The *Saltman* definition is so embarrassingly useless that the judges, anxious to avoid further embarrassment, have simply refused to attempt more helpful definitions. The last refuge of the jurisprudentially destitute is policy: that is where the judges have gone. Disclosure will be prohibited if disclosure in the relevant circumstances would be 'within the mischief which the law as its policy seeks to avoid ...'[7] This is obviously useless too: it comes to no more than saying that disclosure will be found to be wrong if disclosure is wrong.
2.5.3	In relation to information communicated to a doctor by a patient in the course of a professional consultation, the position is clear: unless that information is already in the public domain it will be an actionable breach of confidence to disclose it. Whether information is sufficiently in the public domain for this to be a defence to such an action will be a matter of fact and degree in each case.

---

5   *Stephens v Avery* [1988] 2 WLR 1280; *BSC v Granada Television Ltd* [1981] 1 All ER 417.

6   (1948) 65 RPC 203, at 215.

7   *Argyll v Argyll* [1967] 1 Ch 312, per Ungoed-Thomas J at 330.

2.5.4   The difficult cases arise when a patient has disclosed facts to a doctor other than in the course of a formal consultation, or where a third party tells a doctor something about a patient without realising knowing about the doctor-patient relationship. The English courts have not yet adjudicated on such cases, but when they do, they will be very ready to find that the doctor in such circumstances must maintain confidentiality.

2.5.5   A tale which has gone the rounds (however undesirable a claimant may think it is that it continues to do the rounds), cannot properly be described as confidential. The courts are not in the business of trying to stuff cats back into bags from which they have been let out. Whether information has been sufficiently distributed for it to have lost its confidential nature will always, however, be a matter of fact and degree, and no useful general principles can be stated.

2.5.6   Although the extent of dissemination will always be a factor in the court deciding whether or not the information in question has lost the quality of confidentiality, if the claimant himself has caused the dissemination, the court will be particularly reluctant to do anything about it.[8] This, however, is probably best regarded as an example of the law relating to remedies (in this case injunctions and damages) than about the substantive law of confidentiality.

2.5.7   The courts are reluctant to protect very old information from disclosure. Thus publication of the Crossman diaries, which contained records of Cabinet discussions which were prima facie confidential, was permitted ten years after the events spoken of.[9] This is probably best

---

8   See, for instance, *Lennon v News Group Newspapers Ltd v Twist* [1978] FSR 573; *Woodward v Hutchins* [1977] 2 All ER 751, cp *A-G v Guardian* [1987] 3 All ER 316.

9   See *A-G v Times Newspapers Ltd* [1976] QB 752; Also *A-G v Jonathan Cape Ltd* [1976] 1 QB 752, where Lord Widgery CJ, at p771, said: 'There must ... be a limit in time after which the confidential character of the information, and the duty of the court to restrain publication, will lapse ... It may, of course, be intensely difficult in a particular case, to say at what point the material loses its confidential character, on the ground that publication will no longer undermine the doctrine of Cabinet responsibility ...'

regarded as an example of laches, or of the operation that 'equity is not in vain'. It would be vain to prevent things which did not need preventing.

2.5.8   It does not necessarily follow from this that unconscionable dissemination of information which is already in the public domain will not be actionable, but there have been no English decisions yet where a claimant has won on this basis.[10] An English claimant wishing to argue that there should be liability in these circumstances would presumably have to contend that the doctor owed him some sort of fiduciary responsibility, and that disclosure amounted to an actionable breach of trust.

2.5.9   There are indications that the English courts may be reluctant to refine any further the definition of 'confidential information'. Thus in *R v Department of Health ex p Source Informatics Ltd*[11], a case about the supply of information by pharmacists about prescribers to data collection companies, the Court of Appeal, despite having detailed argument on the issue of whether anonymised information was 'confidential' sidestepped the issue and decided the case simply by asking whether what the pharmacists had done was unconscionable, ie was there a breach or not?

2.5.10   Whether anonymised information is 'confidential information' will really be a question of fact. The question will be whether the anonymising has been sufficiently thorough for it to be possible to identify the claimant as the subject of or the source of the information.

2.6   **Circumstances of confidentiality**

2.6.1   Having failed to produce a workable definition of confidential information, the courts have taken refuge in the idea that they will protect information which has

10 For a Californian example of an action based on further disclosure by a doctor for gain of information disclosed to him in his capacity as a doctor which, by the time of the further disclosure, had already lost, in English terms, its confidential character, see *Moore v Regents of the University of California* (1990) 793 P 2d 479.

11 [2000] Lloyd's Rep Med 76.

not lost the characteristic of confidentiality, when the disclosure to the potential defendant of the information has been in circumstances of confidentiality.

2.6.2   Like elephants, these circumstances are obvious enough when you see them, but difficult to describe. Mostly, in clinical cases, this does not matter.

2.6.3   The vast majority of clinical relationships are relationships which create circumstances of confidentiality. Partly such circumstances are creatures of the parties' expectations. Patients certainly do not expect their doctor to tell the world, or even the diners in the junior doctors' canteen, the intimacies which they braced themselves to tell the doctor. And, as will be seen, the healthcare professionals' own professional organisations do not expect their members to disclose those intimacies.

2.6.4   Thus the number of specifically clinical cases in which 'circumstances of confidentiality' has been in issue is very small: everyone has always taken the existence of those circumstances as read. In case it is necessary to argue about this, though, it should be noted that the courts have prevented the disclosure of confidences between spouses[12], close friends[13] and Cabinet members.[14]

2.6.5   It was argued in *Stephens v Avery* (supra) that unless there was either an enforceable contract or some sort of pre-existing relationship such as doctor and patient or priest and penitent, no legal duty of confidence could be imposed simply by saying that the information was given in confidence. This was rejected. The court said:

'The basis of equitable intervention to protect confidentiality is that it is unconscionable for a person who has received information on the basis that it is confidential subsequently to reveal that information. Although the relationship between the parties is often important in cases where it is said there is an implied as opposed to

12   *Argyll v Argyll* [1967] 1 Ch 302.
13   *Stephens v Avery* [1988] 2 WLR 1280.
14   *A-G v Jonathan Cape Ltd* [1976] 1 QB 752.

express obligation of confidence, the relationship between the parties is not the determining factor. It is the acceptance of the information on the basis that it will be kept secret that affects the conscience of the recipient of the information.'[15]

2.6.6   In most conceivable clinical circumstances the healthcare professional will have accepted the information on the basis that it will be kept secret. It would therefore be unconscionable to disclose it, and the law will generally intervene to prevent such unconscionable disclosure.

2.7   **The 'public interest defence':**
competing public interests

2.7.1   The term 'public interest defence' is commonly used. It refers to the situation when a defendant claims that disclosure, which is prima facie a breach of confidentiality, should not be restrained by the law or condemned by way of an award of damages because the public interest in its disclosure outweighed the public interest in maintaining confidentiality.

2.7.2   The quibble is of little practical significance, but this use of language is legally wrong. It is part of the definition of an actionable breach of confidence that the public interest in disclosure is outweighed by the public interest in maintaining the confidence.

2.7.3   The notion of competing *public* interests is relatively recent. Older cases talked about private interests in maintaining confidences being outweighed by public interests in disclosure. This is an important shift.

2.7.4   The notion of weighing competing public interests is well illustrated by the two cases which follow. They are tremendous worked examples which demonstrate almost everything necessary about the law of clinical confidentiality. They are the most important cases in this book.

---

15 Per Sir Nicholas Browne-Wilkinson V-C at 1286.

2.7.5   *X v Y and others* [1988] 2 All ER 648

The claimant was a health authority. The first defendant was a newspaper reporter employed by the second defendant, a national newspaper.

An employee or employees of the claimant supplied the first defendant with information, extracted from hospital records, which identified two general practitioners who continued in practice despite having AIDS. The second defendant paid for this information.

The claimant obtained an order restraining the defendants from publishing or otherwise making use of the information. After that order was made the second defendant published an article written by the first defendant under the headline 'Scandal of Docs with AIDS', which said that there were doctors with AIDS in England who continued to practice to the knowledge of the Department of Health and Social Security. It implied that the DHSS wanted to suppress this information.

The claimant sought, inter alia, an injunction restraining the defendants from publishing the identity of the two general practitioners. There were other predictable issues relating to contempt of court.

The defendants argued, inter alia, that there was a public interest in disclosure of the identity of the general practitioners, and that that interest outweighed the competing public and private interests in non-disclosure. This argument failed. Rose J balanced the competing interests against one another. He described how he did that exercise:

'I keep in the forefront of my mind the very important public interest in freedom of the press. And I accept that there is some public interest in knowing that which defendants seek to publish ... But in my judgment those public interests are substantially outweighed when measured against the public interests in relation to loyalty and confidentiality both generally and with particular reference to AIDS patients' hospital records. There has been no misconduct by the [claimants]. The records of hospital patients, particularly those suffering from this

appalling condition should, in my judgment, be as confidential as the courts can properly keep them in order
that the [claimants] may be 'free from suspicion that they
are harbouring disloyal employees'. The [claimants]
have 'suffered a grievous wrong in which the defendants
became involved ... with active participation'. The depri-
vation of the public of the information sought to be published will be of minimal significance if the injunction is
granted; for, without it, all the evidence before me
shows that a wide-ranging public debate about AIDS
generally and about its effect on doctors is taking place
among doctors of widely differing views, within and
without the BMA, in medical journals and in many
newspapers, including the *Observer*, the *Sunday Times*
and the *Daily Express*. Indeed, the sterility of the defendants' argument is demonstrated by the edition of the
second defendant's own newspaper dated 22 March
1987. It is there expressly stated, purportedly quoting a
Mr Milligan, that three general practitioners, two of
whom are practising (impliedly in Britain), have AIDS.
Paraphrasing Templeman LJ in the *Schering* case[16], the
facts, in the most limited form now sought to be published, have already been made available and may again
be made available if they are known otherwise than
through the medium of the informer. The risk of identification is only one factor in assessing whether to permit
the use of confidential information. In my judgment to
allow publication in [a] ... restricted form would be to
enable both defendants to procure breaches of confidence and then to make their own selection for publication. This would make a mockery of the law's protection
of confidentiality when no justifying public interest has
been shown. These are the considerations which guide
me, whether my task is properly described as a balancing exercise, or an exercise in judicial judgment, or both
...'[17]

2.7.6   *W v Egdell* [1990] 1 Ch 359

The claimant suffered from paranoid schizophrenia.
In 1974 he killed five people and injured two others.
He pleaded guilty to manslaughter on the grounds of

16 *Schering Chemicals Ltd v Falkman Ltd* [1981] 2 All ER 321.
17 p661.

diminished responsibility. The court ordered that he be detained indefinitely in a secure hospital.

In 1986 the medical officer responsible for the claimant recommended that the claimant be transferred to a regional secure unit. The Secretary of State refused to transfer the claimant. The claimant then applied to a mental health review tribunal. To support his application he obtained a report from the defendant, a consultant psychiatrist. The report did not support the application, but disclosed that the claimant had a long standing and continuing interest in home made bombs and said that the defendant did not agree that the claimant was no longer dangerous. In the light of the defendant's report the claimant withdrew his application to the tribunal. The claimant refused to consent to the disclosure to the hospital's medical officer of the defendant's report. The defendant was not happy about this non-disclosure. He felt that the staff treating the claimant should know about its contents. So he disclosed it to the hospital medical officer, and copies were eventually given to the Secretary of State and the DHSS.

The claimant found out about this disclosure in 1987. He issued proceedings for breach of confidence. The judge at first instance dismissed the claims. The claimant appealed. The Court of Appeal dismissed the appeal, holding:

(a) There was a public interest in maintaining confidentiality as between a doctor and his patient.

(b) That public interest had to be weighed against the public interest in protecting others against crime.

(c) The nature of the claimant's crimes made it a matter of public interest that those responsible for treating and managing him had all the relevant information about him when considering whether he should be released. The contents of the defendant's report were clearly relevant.

(d) The disclosure had been properly made, both when considered in terms of the competing public interest, and also in terms of the General Medical

Council's guidance to doctors faced with this sort of situation.

(e) Only the most compelling circumstances would justify a doctor in doing something which the patient might perceive as being against the patient's interests (eg disclosure of prima facie confidential information) without that patient's consent. But those circumstances pertained here.

(f) Article 8(1) of the European Convention for the Protection of Human Rights may protect an individual against the disclosure of information which is protected by the obligation of professional secrecy. But Article 8(2) envisages that there may be circumstances in which a public authority may legitimately interfere with the exercise of the Article 8(1) right in accordance with the law and where necessary in a democratic society in the interests of public safety or the prevention of crime. Here there was no interference by a public authority. The defendant acted in accordance with the law, and his conduct was necessary in the interests of public safety and the prevention of crime.

2.8   Where keeping a confidence would cloak iniquity

2.8.1   The books are filled with old cases which set out messy exceptions to the general rule that confidences have to be kept. The most famous exception is that there is no right to confidence where confidence would cloak iniquity.[18] But the now well developed idea of competing public interests has made the iniquity-cloaking category more or less redundant. In *Hellewell v Chief Constable of Derbyshire*[19] Laws J pointed out the difficulties inherent in the 'iniquity cloaking' defence. The authorities, for instance, were confused about whether or not the iniquity had to be proved, or whether it was enough

---

18 See, for instance, *Gartside v Outram* (1856) 26 LJ Ch 113.
19 [1995] 4 All ER 473. This case was an unsuccessful attempt by an offender to restrain the police from issuing his photograph to local shopkeepers as part of a Shop Watch scheme.

to show that there was reasonable suspicion of it. It made more sense, he said, to analyse confidentiality problems in terms of the competing public interests. That is the method which has been used since.

2.9   **Looking at it another way: Unconscionable behaviour**

2.9.1   There are signs that the courts are reverting more and more to old fashioned equitable principles. Thus in *R v Department of Health ex p Source Informatics Ltd*[20], Simon Brown LJ said, having reviewed the authorities:

> 'To my mind the one clear and consistent theme emerging from all these authorities is this: the confidant is placed under a duty of good faith to the confider and the touchstone by which to judge the scope of his duty and whether or not it has been fulfilled or breached is his own conscience, no more and no less. One asks, therefore, on the facts of this case: would a reasonable pharmacist's conscience be troubled by the proposed use to be made of patients' prescriptions? Would he think that by entering [the data collection agency's] scheme he was breaking his customers' confidence, making unconscientious use of the information they provide? ... The concern of the law is to protect the confider's personal privacy. That and that alone is the right at issue in this case. The patient has no proprietorial claim to the prescription form or to the information it contains. Of course he can bestow or withhold his custom as he pleases – the pharmacist, note, has no such right: he is by law bound to dispense to whoever presents a prescription. But that gives the patient no property in the information and no right to control its use provided only and always that his privacy is not put at risk ... This appeal concerns, as all agree, the application of a broad principle of equity. I propose its resolution on a similarly broad basis ... I would stand back from the many detailed arguments addressed to us and hold simply that pharmacists' consciences ought not reasonably to be troubled by cooperation with [the data collection agency's] proposed scheme. The patient's privacy will have been safeguarded, not invaded. The pharmacist's

---

20 [2000] Lloyd's Rep: Med 76. The facts are outlined at paragraph 2.5.9 above.

duty of confidence will not have been breached.'[21]

2.9.2   There is no real inconsistency between this approach and the public interest balancing approach. The courts will assume that clinicians' consciences would be troubled by disclosure in circumstances where the public interest in disclosure did not outweigh the   public interest in non-disclosure.

2.10   **The relevance of the codes of the professional organisations**

2.10.1   *Egdell*[22] referred to the General Medical Council's ('GMC's') guidelines as helpful in deciding whether there had been an actionable breach of confidence. But it did not explain why they are helpful.

2.10.2   The guidelines set out what the public can legitimately expect of their doctors. The extent of the obligation to keep confidences is, as noted above, related closely to what the doctors know is expected of them. To use the old equitable language, it would be unconscionable for a doctor to disclose something when he knows the patient expects him not to disclose it.

The guidelines are drafted with the benefit of medical knowledge about what is clinically practicable which lay judges will not necessarily have. They therefore define what type and what extent of guarantee of confidentiality doctors can realistically offer.

2.10.3   In practice the guidelines of the professional regulatory organisations are always referred to in informed debates on clinical confidentiality. It would be unusual for a court to find that a clinician who had acted within his own professional code to be guilty of an actionable breach of confidence. Conversely, however, a clinician whose conduct would be rubber stamped by a civil court might still find himself censured by the GMC.

2.10.4   Most clinical confidentiality cases which come to court involve doctors. The relevant GMC guidelines[23] are

21   Pp82-83.
22   Supra.
23   See Appendix 1.

extremely explicit, well drafted, and legally literate, with many examples which reflect the principles in decided cases. Most of the realistically conceivable problems in the law of confidentiality are anticipated and dealt with there. The guidelines of some of the other regulatory organisations are not so explicit. The GMC's guidelines provide a very good, practical guide as to what the courts are likely to find acceptable. Sometimes they demand more of doctors than the courts are likely to do (for instance in insisting that the duty of confidentiality survives a patient's death)[24], but for most practical purposes are likely to be co-extensive with the law. It is therefore suggested that the GMC guidelines are used as a manual of the law of confidentiality. Where the GMC guidelines cover situations analogous to those in issue where another healthcare profession is involved, the courts are likely to find the analogy helpful. So where (for instance), the guidelines produced by the General Council and Register of Osteopaths are silent or insufficiently explicit on a matter pertaining to confidentiality, look at the GMC's guidelines for comparable situations. One area where caution needs to be exercised, though, is in relation to the GMC guidelines in the *Confidentiality* booklet about disclosure for the purposes of research. Guideline 16[25] states that where a patient's consent to the use of confidential information for research cannot be obtained, a 'research ethics committee' should decide whether the public interest in the research outweighs the right to confidentiality. Presumably this applies to a situation where consent cannot be obtained because the patient is dead or cannot be traced. But this guideline gives to an ethics committee the judicial job of balancing public interests. The court may resent this usurping of its function, and differ sufficiently from the conclusion of the committee to find that notwithstanding the com-

---

24 See paragraph 2.3.2 above.
25 See Appendix 1.

mittee's endorsement of disclosure, there has been an actionable breach of confidentiality.

2.10.5   *The scope of the GMC's guidelines* (the references are to page numbers in this book):
    – General principles of confidentiality: p85;
    – Disclosure of confidential information with the patient's consent: p86;
        – disclosure within teams;
        – disclosure to employers and insurance companies;
    – Disclosure of information without the patient's consent: p87;
        – disclosure in the patient's medical interests;
        – disclosure after a patient's death;
    – Disclosure for medical teaching, medical research and medical audit: p89;
    – Disclosure in the interests of others: p89;
        – patients continuing to drive when medically unfit to do so;
        – colleague putting patients at risk;
        – the prevention or detection of serious crime;
    – Disclosure in connection with judicial or other proceedings: p90;
    – Disclosure to tax inspectors: p90;

2.11   **Special cases: (1) Children**

2.11.1   Doctors owe a duty of confidentiality to patients who are children just as they do to any other patient. But the duty of confidentiality cannot be considered in isolation from the other duty – to give the child appropriate medical care. Because of the way the law of consent works, parents will need to be consulted about the medical care of a child who cannot validly give consent to the treatment proposed. That consultation will of course necessarily entail the disclosure of confidential information. It is therefore necessary to consider when a minor can validly consent to or refuse treatment. The law is contained in the case of *Gillick v West Norfolk & Wisbech AHA*[26] and in s8 of the Family Law Reform Act 1969.

---

26 [1985] 3 All ER 402.

2.11.2   In *Gillick* Lord Scarman said[27] that as a matter of law a minor has the capacity to consent to medical treatment:

'... when the child achieves a sufficient understanding and intelligence to enable him or her to understand fully what is proposed.'

Whether the child has that understanding and intelligence is a question of fact in each case.

2.11.3   It is now clear that the child must also be capable of understanding the consequences of a failure to treat.[28]

2.11.4   By s8 of the Family Law Reform Act 1969:

'(1) The consent of a minor who has attained the age of 16 years to any surgical, medical or dental treatment which, in the absence of consent, would constitute a trespass to his person, shall be as effective as it would be if he were of full age; and where a minor has by virtue of this section given an effective consent to any treatment it shall not be necessary to obtain any consent for it from his parent or guardian.

(2) In this section "surgical, medical or dental treatment" includes any procedure undertaken for the purposes of diagnosis, and this section applies to any procedure (including, in particular, the administration of an anaesthetic) which is ancillary to any treatment as it applies to that treatment).

(3) Nothing in this section shall be construed as making ineffective any consent which would have been effective if this section had not been enacted.'

2.11.5   This was considered in *W (A Minor) (Medical Treatment: Court's Jurisdiction)*.[29] A girl, aged 16, suffered from anorexia nervosa. The local authority sought leave to remove her to an establishment where she might be treated and leave to treat her without her consent. It was held that:

---

27   At p423.
28   Per Lord Donaldson MR in *Re R (a Minor) (Wardship: Medical Treatment)* [1991] 4 All ER 177.
29   [1992] 3 Med LR 317.

(a) The Family Law Reform Act 1969 s8 made consent to medical treatment by a girl aged 16 as effective as if she were of full age;

(b) The section is of no significance at all where a minor between the ages of 16 and 18 has *refused* to give consent.

(c) Where a minor is *Gillick* competent those with parental responsibility could not override its decision to refuse treatment.

(d) The statutory right does not extend to the donation of blood or organs.

2.11.6   Where, according to these criteria, a minor is not competent to consent to whatever is proposed, such disclosure as is necessary in order lawfully to obtain consent will not be unlawful.

2.12   **Special cases: (2) Persons under a disability**

2.12.1   Most patients suffering from a mental disorder are subject to the same rules as other adults so far as the obtaining of consent is concerned.

2.12.2   Sections 56-64 of the Mental Health Act 1983 contain various provisions relating to consent to treatment for patients who are liable to be detained under those sections. But the only treatment authorised by those sections in the absence of consent is treatment for the relevant mental disorder.

2.12.3   Accordingly, if a patient liable to be detained under those sections refuses to give his consent to treatment for a medical condition unrelated to his mental disorder, the treatment will be illegal unless the doctrine of necessity applies.

2.12.4   Note that in relation to the medical treatment of patients with mental disorder, the courts are prepared to construe the doctrine of necessity very widely: see *F v West Berkshire HA*.[30] This related to the sterilisation of a 36-year-old woman who suffered from serious mental disability. Lord Brandon concluded that an operation or other treatment performed on adult patients who

---

30 [1989] 2 All ER 545.

are incapable of consenting would be lawful provided that it is in the best interests of the patients. It will be in their best interests:

'... if, but only if, it is carried out in order either to save their lives or to ensure improvement or prevent deterioration in their physical or mental health.'[31]

What, though, apart, from torture or perverted sexual gratification, would motivate a doctor other than the motives described by Lord Brandon? The doctrine is very wide indeed.

2.12.5 Controversially, the *Bolam* test was applied to the issue of how the patient's best interests should be determined.

2.12.6 The courts are very ready to find that patients are suffering from mental disability. The classic example is in *Re L (Patient: Non-consensual Treatment)*[32] (re fear of needles).

Mental patients who cannot validly consent to treatment according to the criteria above cannot complain about a breach of confidence when the breach has been committed in the course of jumping through the legal hoops necessary to make the proposed treatment lawful from the standpoint of the law of consent.

2.13 **Is detriment a necessary ingredient of an actionable breach of confidence?**

2.13.1 It depends who is trying to establish the breach of confidence. Different rules apply to the Crown, and quite right too.

2.13.2 Where the claimant is a body other than the Crown, it is not necessary to show detriment in order to establish an actionable breach of confidence. Alternatively the mere fact of disclosure is itself the detriment. In *A-G v Guardian Newspapers (No 2)*[33] Lord Keith said:

'As a general rule it is in the public interest that confidences should be respected, and the encouragement of

---

31 At p551.
32 [1997] 8 Med LR 217.
33 [1990] AC 109.

such respect may in itself constitute a sufficient ground for recognising and enforcing the obligation of confidence even where the confider can point to no specific detriment to himself. Information about a person's private and personal affairs may be of a nature which shows him up in a favourable light and would by no means expose him to criticism. The anonymous donor of a very large sum to a very worthy cause has his own reasons for wishing to remain anonymous, which are unlikely to be discreditable. He should surely be in a position to restrain disclosure in breach of confidence of his identity in connection with the donation. So I would think it a sufficient detriment to the confider that information given in confidence is to be disclosed to persons whom he would prefer not to know of it, even though the disclosure would not be harmful to him in any positive way.'[34]

2.13.3   The analogy with defamation is obviously good. Lord Keith is saying that a breach of confidence is actionable per se without proof of special damage. Thus a threat of unlawful disclosure will entitle a claimant to an injunction. Whether it is necessary to show detriment in order to establish a claim for more than nominal damages is examined in Chapter 2.

2.13.4   But where the Crown is seeking to restrain disclosure the position is different. In *A-G v Guardian Newspapers (No 2)*[35] Lord Keith said:

'Insofar as the Crown acts to prevent such disclosure or to seek redress for it on confidentiality grounds, it must necessarily, in my opinion, be in a position to show that the disclosure is likely to damage or has damaged the public interest. How far the Crown has to go in order to show this must depend on the circumstances of each case.'[36]

---

34 At p256 Lord Griffiths, at p270, thought that detriment, or potential detriment, did need to be established, but he did not dissent from Lord Keith's assumption about what could amount to detriment. Lord Goff was coy, but in hinting that whether or not there was a requirement of detriment might depend on the width of detriment, was winking at Lord Keith's comment. But cp *Coco v AN Clark (Engineering) Ltd* [1969] RPC 41.

35 Supra.

36 At p256.

2.13.5   In *Lord Advocate v The Scotsman*[37] Lord Templeman said that when deciding whether or not the Crown would be granted an injunction, the court should use the same criteria as when deciding whether a criminal offence of wrongful disclosure under the Official Secrets Act 1989 has been committed.[38]

2.14   **Breach of confidence actions and the Data Protection Act 1998**
The 1998 Act has the potential to revolutionise breach of clinical confidentiality cases. The revolution has not yet happened, and the common law will not be ousted, but there is certainly the potential for a lot of fundamental change in the way that confidentiality cases are framed. See Chapter 5 below.

2.15   **Negligent disclosure and non-disclosure**

2.15.1   The common law of negligence generally fills the gaps where other remedies (eg contractual) provide no assistance. There is no clear view as to whether the English law of negligence provides a remedy for either (i) negligent disclosure or (ii) negligent non-disclosure of what would usually be regarded as confidential information.

2.15.2   The short answer to (i) above is that no English court has to date provided a remedy for negligent disclosure of confidential information. Whilst this may sound odd, given that it could hardly be regarded as 'reasonable' or 'acceptable' practice to unlawfully disclose confidential information, and whilst harm may well be reasonably foreseeable, a claimant can and must at present rely on the doctrine of breach of confidence.

2.15.3   The position as to (ii) is particularly interesting where it is claimed that confidential information should have been disclosed to prevent harm to a third party (by disclosing, eg the criminal intent of the patient) or indeed to the claimant himself (by disclosing a serious

---

37 [1990] 1 AC 812.
38 See pp823-4 of *Lord Advocate v The Scotsman*, and the Official Secrets Act 1989 ss1(4) and 5(3).

undiagnosed condition). English courts have stead-fastly refused to allow such claims to date, even in tear-jerking cases.[39] The extent of the duty of a doctor who examines another to whom he owes no duty of care by reason of a doctor-patient relationship (eg defendant expert witness examining claimant to prepare a condition and prognosis report or police surgeon examining a prisoner to determine fitness for detention) is no more than not to make matters worse by causing actual physical harm during the course of the examination. However, it has recently been said, albeit *obiter*, that:

> 'It also seems to me that it is at least arguable that where a [doctor] carries out an examination and discovers that the person being examined has, say, a serious condition which needs immediate treatment, he or she owes a duty to that person to inform him or her of the position.'[40]

It will be interesting to see if this dictum is adopted.

---

39   Eg *Palmer v Tees HA* [1998] Lloyd's Rep Med 447, QBD and [1999] Lloyd's Rep Med 351, CA.

40   *Re N* [1999] Lloyd's Rep Med 257, CA, per Clarke LJ at p263.

Chapter 3
The Impact of Statute on the Law of Confidentiality

3.1   **Introduction**

3.1.1   Statutes and statutory instruments can affect the common law obligation of confidence in three ways: (i) they can make disclosure of confidential information compulsory where that would otherwise be a breach of the common law obligation; (ii) they can make disclosure of confidential information permissible (subject to the holder's discretion) where that would otherwise be a breach of the common law obligation; (iii) they can reinforce the common law obligation by providing penalties for unauthorised use or disclosure (see Chapter 5 for the Data Protection Act 1998).

3.1.2   This Chapter deals briefly with the major areas in which statutes and statutory instruments other than the Human Rights Act have affected confidentiality. It is clear that in general there are obvious policy grounds for requiring or permitting disclosure in each area.

3.2   **Abortion**

3.2.1   The Abortion Regulations 1991[41] require any registered medical practitioner who terminates a pregnancy in England or Wales to provide the Chief Medical Officer with notice of termination together with any

---

41 SI 1991/499.

other information which the prescribed form of notification specifies.

3.2.2 These Regulations prohibit further disclosure of the notice or specified information to the Chief Medical Officer other than for the purposes set out in Article 5 of the Regulations, which include: (i) to the Director of Public Prosecutions or a police officer in connection with offences relating to abortion; (ii) to a court in connection with criminal proceedings; (iii) for bone fide scientific research; (iv) to the medical practitioner who terminated the pregnancy or any medical practitioner with the consent of the woman whose pregnancy was terminated; (v) to the GMC in connection with proceedings for serious professional misconduct.

3.2.3 Wilful contravention or wilful failure to comply with these requirements is an offence.

3.3 **Public Health**

3.3.1 The Public Health (Control of Disease) Act 1984 requires a registered medical practitioner to notify the proper officer of the local authority whenever he becomes aware or suspects that a patient whom he attends is suffering from one of a list of notifiable diseases. The obligation is deemed sufficiently important that failure to notify the proper officer with the prescribed information is a criminal offence punishable with a fine.

3.3.2 The Public Health (Infectious Diseases) Regulations 1998[42] supplement the above Act with a wide range of infectious diseases which must be reported. The full list is: acute encephalitis, acute meningitis, acute poliomyelitis, anthrax, cholera, diphtheria, dysentery, food poisoning, leprosy, leptospirosis, malaria, measles, meningococcal septicaemia, mumps, ophthalmia, neonatorum, paratyphoid fever, plague, rabies, relapsing fever, rubella, scarlet fever, smallpox, tetanus, tuberculosis, typhoid fever, typhus, viral haemorrhagic

42 SI 1988/1546.

fever, viral hepatitis, whooping cough and yellow fever.

3.3.3   The National Health Service (Venereal Diseases) Regulations 1974[43] prohibit the disclosure by Regional and District Health Authorities of any information obtained by their staff with respect to persons examined or treated for any sexually transmitted disease shall not be disclosed except to a medical practitioner in connection with, and for the purposes of, treatment for the disease or preventing the spread of the disease. These Regulations permit disclosure for the purposes of treatment to the patient's GP where care is shared between hospital and GP. However, the Regulations appear to permit disclosure for the purposes of prevention or spread in the absence of consent or even where the patient expressly refuses to give consent (the obvious example being to protect the patient's partner). In addition, the courts have so far assumed that 'sexually transmitted disease' refers to the means by which the disease is usually transmitted, rather than the means by which it was in fact transmitted in the instant case.[44] HIV positive patients who contracted the virus through, eg an infected blood donation will not be covered by the Regulations.

3.4   **Births**

3.4.1   Any person in attendance on a mother is obliged to notify the district medical officer of the birth of any child born dead or alive after the 28th week of pregnancy.[45] It is possible to discharge this obligation by instructing someone else to notify the birth.

3.5   **Fertility treatment**

3.5.1   It is not within the scope of this book to consider in detail the topic of human fertilisation. The area is heavily circumscribed by statute (the Human Fertilisation and Embryology Act 1990 as amended).

---

43 SI 1974/29.
44 *X v Y* [1988] 2 All ER 648.
45 National Health Service Act 1977, s124(4); National Health Service (Notification of Births and Deaths) Regulations 1982, SI 1982/286.

3.5.2   It is only necessary to draw attention to the 1990 Act and also to the Human Fertilisation and Embryology (Disclosure of Information) Act 1992. A distinction is drawn between statutory and non-statutory information. The two Acts regulate the disclosure of information by and to the Human Fertilisation and Embryology Authority and by and to its licence-holders.

3.6   **Investigation and prevention of crime**

3.6.1   The Police and Criminal Evidence Act 1984 ('PACE 1984') gives the police certain rights to gain entry to property in order to carry out searches on obtaining a warrant from a justice of the peace. Some of the material which the police may be interested in may be material which would usually be regarded as confidential. Where this material is defined by PACE 1984 to be 'excluded material', a constable may only gain access and seize it by applying to a circuit judge. Excluded material includes: (i) personal records acquired or created in the course of a trade, business, profession or other occupation or for the purpose of any paid or unpaid office *and which he holds in confidence*.[46] Personal records include any documentary and other records relating to a person's physical and mental health.[47]

3.6.2   Hospital records of patients' admission and discharge from a mental hospital have been held to constitute 'personal records' because they are records 'relating to' a persons's 'mental health'.[48]

3.6.3   The good intentions of the above are rather undermined by the principle that the police may seize excluded material without a court order if they are lawfully on premises for another purpose, provided they have reasonable grounds for believing that it is relevant evidence in relation to their investigation

---

46 Section 11(1)(a).
47 Section 12(a).
48 *R v Cardiff Crown Court, ex parte Kellam*, DC, The Times 3 May 1993.

and that it is necessary to seize it to prevent it from being destroyed.[49]

3.6.4   The Road Traffic Act 1988 provides that, where the driver of a vehicle or the rider of a bicycle is alleged to be guilty of a road traffic offence 'any other person shall if required ... give such information which it is in his power to give and may lead to the identification of the driver'.[50] Rather surprisingly this section has been held to apply to a doctor who receives information in confidence from a patient, whose criminal conviction for refusal to disclose the information (obtained in the course of his professional duties) was upheld by the Court of Appeal.

3.6.5   The Prevention of Terrorism (Temporary Provisions) Act 1989[51] makes it an offence for anyone with certain information about terrorists to refuse to disclose it to the police.[52]

3.7   **Requests for medical records by defence solicitors**

3.7.1   Occasionally the defence team in a criminal case will seek disclosure of medical records held by a medical practitioner. Usually the patient (usually but not exclusively the victim of the alleged offence) will have withheld consent to disclosure.

3.7.2   The proper course of action in such circumstances is for the defence to issue a witness summons under the *Criminal Procedure (Attendance of Witnesses) Act 1965*.[53] The summons should be addressed to the general practitioner or relevant NHS Trust/Health Authority as relevant. Rules of Court explain how the application for a witness summons must be made.[54] Usually the witness will object to disclosing the medical records voluntarily (particularly where no patient consent has been given) and a hearing will be requested. Often the

---

49 Section 19.
50 Section 170(b).
51 Renewed annually since 1989.
52 Sections 18 and 18A.
53 As amended by the Criminal Procedure and Investigations Act 1996.
54 Crown Court Rules 1982 as amended.

judge will wish to consider the medical records himself before ordering disclosure in the context of the defence submissions as to their (actual or potential) relevance in the light of the issues in the case.

3.7.3   A witness summons may be set aside on the grounds of lack or particularity, inadmissibility, immateriality or public interest immunity. It is for the defence to persuade the court that the records ought to be disclosed. Where a doctor wishes to make such a plea he should be separately represented.

Chapter 4
Disclosure Where Litigation is Contemplated or Proceeding

4.1.	**Introduction**
4.1.1	The law relating to the procedure to be followed when ligation is contemplated or proceeding has recently been rewritten. The Civil Procedure Rules ('CPR') have replaced the old Rules of the Supreme Court and the County Court Rules which governed procedure.
4.1.2	This chapter is not an essay on the law of disclosure. It deals only with issues of confidentiality which arise in relation to litigation.
4.2.	**Confidentiality in the disclosure process**
4.2.1	Confidentiality is important in the law of disclosure for the following reasons:

(a) A claimant is generally taken to have consented to the disclosure of such otherwise confidential information as will properly be disclosed in the course of or in anticipation of litigation. There are various legal analyses of this situation. Probably the best way of looking at it is to say that the claimant, by intimating litigation or issuing proceedings, waives a right to confidentiality and impliedly agrees to disclosure to those persons involved in the course of litigation who would ordinarily see the confidential information.

(b)   The assertion of confidentiality can sometimes bar the disclosure of prima facie discloseable documents.

4.2.2   It follows from 2.1(a) that since disclosure is only authorised to the people to whom disclosure is necessary then, unless and until the material becomes public knowledge in the course of public court proceedings, the parties running the disclosure process must take care to avoid unauthorized people getting sight of the information. Sometimes, if the court makes an order, even if the material is used in open court, subsequent disclosure may be restricted.

4.2.3   The care which must be taken will depend on the circumstances. There is confidential information and confidential information. Not all material need necessarily be kept under lock and key. Some will. In big cases more people will be involved in the disclosure process, (and will therefore be impliedly authorised to see confidential information), than in little ones. It is necessary to understand the discovery procedure in order to understand the limits of the implied authority. That is why the procedure is outlined skeletally below.

4.3.   **Disclosure before litigation has begun**

4.3.1   In practice, medical records are often simply requested and informally disclosed.

4.3.2   The court can make orders for the pre-action disclosure of documents by a prospective party in any kind of proceedings.[55]

4.3.3   In clinical negligence and personal injury cases the formal pre-action machinery is now much less significant than it used to be. This is because of two of Woolf's creatures: the pre-action protocols for personal injury claims and for the resolution of clinical disputes.

4.3.4   These pre-action protocols are enforced by the court with the threat of draconian costs and interest penalties for non-compliance.

55   See s34 Supreme Court Act 1981, s53 *County Courts Act 1984*, and CPR Parts 25.1(i) and 31.16.

4.3.5   The pre-action protocol for the resolution of clinical disputes prescribes a procedure which will often raise issues of clinical confidentiality. Under the heading 'Obtaining the Health Records' it states:

'3.7 Any request by the patient or their adviser should:

- provide sufficient information to alert the healthcare provider where an adverse outcome has been serious or had serious consequences.

- be as specific as possible about the records which are required.

3.8   Requests for copies of the patient's clinical records should be made using the Law Society and Department of Health approved standard forms ... adapted as necessary.

3.9   The copy records should be provided within 40 days of the request and for a cost not exceeding the charges permissible under the Access to Health Records Act 1990 (currently a maximum of £10 plus photocopying and postage).

3.10 In the rare circumstances that the healthcare provider is in difficulty in complying with the request within 40 days, the problem should be explained quickly and details given of what is being done to resolve it.

3.11 It will not be practicable for healthcare providers to investigate in detail every case where records are requested. But healthcare providers should adopt a policy on which cases will be investigated ...

3.12 If the healthcare provider fails to provide the health records within 40 days, the patient or their provider can then apply to the court for an order for pre-action disclosure. The new Civil Procedure Rules should make pre-action applications to the court easier. The court will also have the power to impose costs sanctions for unreasonable delay in providing records.

3.13 If either the patient or the healthcare provider considers additional health records are required from a third party, in the first instance these should be requested by or through the patient. Third party healthcare providers are expected to cooperate. The Civil Procedure Rules will enable patients and healthcare providers to apply to the court for pre-action disclosure by third parties.'

4.4. **Disclosure in the course of litigation: General**

4.4.1 The overriding principle is that the only documents disclosed should be those whose disclosure is 'necessary'. This was a reaction to expensive, lengthy and tedious discovery exercises. The old law said that documents satisfying the famous Peruvian Guano test should be disclosed. That has been overruled.

4.5. **Standard disclosure**

4.5.1 By CPR Part 31.5:

'(1) An order to give disclosure is an order to give standard disclosure unless the court directs otherwise.

(2) The court may dispense with or limit standard disclosure.

(3) The parties may agree in writing to dispense with or to limit standard disclosure ...'

4.5.2 By CPR Part 31.6:

'Standard disclosure requires a party to disclose only

(a) the documents on which he relies; and

(b) the documents which –

(i) adversely affect his own case;

(ii) adversely affect another party's case; or

(iii) support another party's case; and

(iv) the documents which he is required to disclose by a relevant practice direction.'

4.5.3 So, by CPR Part 31.5, there is an assumption that there will be standard disclosure. If there is a departure from standard disclosure, it will generally be a departure in the direction of disclosing less than standard disclosure would have given. There is provision in the CPR for the disclosure of more than what standard disclosure can give (this is implicit in the words 'unless the court directs otherwise' in CPR 31.5), but in practice submissions that one should get more rather than less are likely to be doomed.

4.6.   **Orders for disclosure against non-parties to litigation**

4.6.1   The procedure is in CPR Part 31.17. This is only a procedural section. The power to compel non-parties to produce documents comes from s34 of the Supreme Court Act 1981 and s53 of the County Courts Act 1984.

4.6.2   These orders are quite often relevant to doctors. Where a doctor is asked to disclose information, but is uncertain about whether that disclosure would amount to a breach of confidence, the doctor will often refuse to disclose the information unless ordered by the court to do so. Of course there can be no actionable breach of confidence where disclosure has been ordered by the court.

4.7.   **The use which can be made of disclosed material**

4.7.1   The courts are concerned that material disclosed in the litigation process might be abused. The court has an inherent jurisdiction to do whatever is necessary to stop that abuse. Thus, for instance, it may allow disclosure subject to implied undertakings as to the people who will see the information.[56] This jurisdiction is under-used in medical cases. A lot of fears about insensitive broadcasting of confidential information could be allayed by judges extracting undertakings about the range of the broadcasting.

4.7.2   The basic rule about the use of disclosed information while proceedings are going on is set out at paragraphs 2.1 and 2.2 above. The court is very ready to construe implied undertakings to this effect in order to enforce the rule.

4.7.3   Lots of court-clogging problems arose about the use which could be made of disclosed documents for purposes other than the proceedings in which the disclosure occurred. The law is now set out simply in CPR Part 31.22. This states:

---

56 See, for instance, *Church of Scientology v DHSS* [1979] 1 WLR 723: *Halcon International Ltd Inc v Shell Transport & Trading Co* [1979] RPC 97.

'(1) A party to whom a document has been disclosed may use the document only for the purpose of the proceedings in which it is disclosed, except where:

(a) the document has been read to or by the court, or referred to, at a hearing which has been held in public;

(b) the court gives permission;

(c) the party who disclosed the document and the person to whom the document belongs agree.

(2) The court may make an order restricting or prohibiting the use of a document which has been disclosed, even where the document has been read to or by the court, or referred to, at a hearing which has been held in public.

(3) An application for such an order may be made:

(a) by a party; or

(b) by any person to whom the document belongs.'

4.7.4   This makes the position in civil proceedings clear. The position about documents disclosed in the course of criminal proceedings is not clear. Probably, though, a court would consider that there was an implied undertaking not to use documents so disclosed for any purposes other than those of the criminal proceedings in which they were disclosed.[57]

4.8.   **Withholding disclosure in the public interest**

4.8.1   **What is public interest immunity?**

4.8.1.1   The best general statement is in *R v Chief Constable of West Midlands, ex p Wiley*[58], where Lord Templeman said:

'Public interest immunity is a ground for refusing to disclose a document which is relevant and material to the determination of issues involved in civil or criminal proceedings. A claim to public interest immunity can only be justified if the public interest in preserving the

---

57 *Taylor v Director of the Serious Fraud Office* [1999] 2 AC 177: cp *Mahon v Rahn* [1998] QB 424.

58 [1994] 3 WLR 433.

confidentiality of the document outweighs the public interest in securing justice.'[59]

4.8.1.2   The doctrine of public interest immunity turns the holders of documents which might be immune from disclosure into guardians of the public interest. That means that if disclosure of a document would prima facie be damaging to the public interest, the holder of that document cannot simply waive immunity. He is under a duty to assert that immunity and, if the assertion is contested, let the court decide whether the assertion is rightly made.

4.8.2   **How can public interest immunity arise in clinical cases?**

4.8.2.1   It has long been established that documents, the disclosure of which may compromise the proper functioning of the public service, may attract immunity.[60] A number of cases try to identify classes of documents which will always attract immunity, and to give guidance on how to decide whether individual documents which do not fall into one of the established immune classes, are nonetheless immune from disclosure. But it is also well established that the categories of public interest immunity are not closed[61]: the idea of public interest immunity continues to evolve to fit changing legal and social circumstances. One of the established categories of documents which may attract immunity (we are talking here of broad analytic categories, not of class immunity), is documents whose disclosure would discourage the free flow of information which it is important, for official purposes, should flow. This is the category into which asserters of immunity in relation to medical documents have to try to squeeze the documents, unless they wish to invoke *D v NSPCC*[62] and create a new category of their own.

---

59   At p436.
60   See *Conway v Rimmer* [1968] AC 910.
61   *D v NSPCC* [1977] 1 All ER 589.
62   Supra.

4.8.2.2   Official medical records have been held to attract immunity on this basis. Thus the report of a doctor to the Home Office on an exhumed murder victim was held to be immune from disclosure,[63] as were medical reports on the mental condition of a prisoner who attacked another prisoner.[64] Probably the modern law is best represented by *R v Secretary of State for the Home Department, ex p Benson.*[65] Here, a medical report was produced on a prisoner serving a life sentence. It was considered by the Home Secretary in relation to the length of the sentence which the prisoner should serve. The prisoner sought disclosure of the report. The Home Secretary claimed public interest immunity, arguing that liability to production would inhibit the candour of reports, and that this would not be in the public interest. This was rejected.

4.8.2.3   But it seems much more strongly arguable that liability to production would inhibit the candour of patients in releasing confidences to their doctors. It may be, then, that ordinary medical records can attract immunity. That is certainly the conclusion in several cases.

4.8.2.4   In *R v K*[66], K was the defendant in a criminal trial. He applied for production of a video of an interview which was made for therapeutic purposes at a children's hospital. The hospital objected to disclosure of the video on the ground of public interest immunity. The trial judge did not view the tape, but accepted the hospital's submission. The defendant was convicted, appealed, and said that non-disclosure amounted to a material irregularity, and further that the judge should have seen the video tape before making his ruling.

4.8.2.5   The Court of Appeal held that where there was a claim for public interest immunity, the court had to balance

63 *Williams v Star Newspaper Co Ltd* (1908) 24 LTR 297.
64 *Ellis v Home Office* [1953] 2 QB 135 cp *Leigh v Gladstone* (1909) 26 TLR 139 (report of a prison doctor to the Governor not immune from disclosure).
65 Unreported, 1 November 1988. Cited in *R v Secretary of State for the Home Department ex p Duggan* [1994] 3 All ER 277 at 285.
66 (1993) 97 Cr App Rep 342.

the competing public interests of confidentiality in the video and of fairness to the defendant. The judge should have viewed the video, but if he had, he would have declined to order disclosure. Accordingly the appeal was dismissed.

4.8.2.6   The courts have identified a number of classes of documents to which public interest attaches. They include, predictably, documents relating to national security. But it has not been finally decided at High Court or Court of Appeal level whether any of the documents routinely at issue in clinical cases attract class immunity. It seems, though, very doubtful whether they do. Probably the right result was reached in *Mercer v St Helens & Knowsley Hospitals NHS Trust*.[67]

4.8.2.7   In this case, P was a patient of an NHS Trust. He made various complaints to the Trust management. An independent review was conducted by two consultants. They had available the relevant medical notes and evidence, both written and oral, from P and from various medical staff involved in P's treatment. P sought copies of the documentation available to the consultants, and a copy of their final report. The documentation was in the hands of the RHA. The RHA asserted public interest immunity, saying that 'class immunity' attached to all the documents sought.

4.8.2.8   The court held that class immunity had not been established, but that public interest immunity might attach to individual documents or parts of documents.

4.8.2.9   The question may arise whether public interest immunity can be invoked by private organisations, such as private hospitals. The answer, although not conclusively decided in this country, must be yes. It is inconceivable that documents in class A, which would attract public interest immunity were they to be generated in an NHS hospital, would not attract immunity in a private hospital. The question which the court would ask in such a situation would not be: 'Is the party assert-

---

67 (1995) CLY 95/4124 (County Court): cp *Copp v Chief Constable of Avon and Somerset Police* (1997) CLY 97/463 (County Court).

ing public interest immunity properly speaking a public body?', but 'Would the disclosure of the documents injure the public interest?' This is the question which needs to be answered in any consideration of public interest immunity. If the answer to it is 'Yes', then the test to be applied in deciding whether they should nonetheless be disclosed will be the old confidentiality one: 'Does the public interest in disclosure outweigh the public interest in non-disclosure?' So for all practical purposes the substantive law of public interest immunity is identical to the substantive law of confidentiality.

4.8.3   **Procedure**

4.8.3.1   If a claim of public interest immunity suggests itself, ask if the documents to which it might attach are really relevant to the issues between the parties. In practice the courts will go out of their way to dodge the issue of public interest immunity by finding a way to try the action with unappealable fairness without reference to the issues to which the document goes.

4.8.3.2   The procedure is set out in CPR 31.19. It is self-explanatory. It states:

'(1) A person may apply, without notice, for an order permitting him to withhold disclosure of a document on the ground that disclosure would damage the public interest.

(2) Unless the court orders otherwise, an order of the court under paragraph (1)

(a) must not be served on any other person; and

(b) must not be open to inspection by any person.

(3) A person who wishes to claim that he has a right or a duty to withhold inspection of a document, or part of a document must state in writing –

(a) that he has such a right or duty; and

(b) the grounds on which he claims that right or duty.

(4) The statement referred to in paragraph (3) must be made

      (a) in the list in which the document is disclosed; or

      (b) if there is no list, to the person wishing to inspect the document.

(5) A party may apply to the court to decide whether a claim made under paragraph (3) should be upheld.

(6) For the purpose of deciding an application under paragraph (1) (application to withhold disclosure) or paragraph (3) (claim to withhold inspection) the court may:

      (a) require the person seeking to withhold disclosure or inspection of a document to produce that document to the court; and

      (b) invite any person, whether or not a party, to make representations.

(7) An application under paragraph (1) or paragraph (5) must be supported by evidence.

(8) This Part does not affect any rule of law which permits or requires a document to be withheld from disclosure or inspection on the grounds that its disclosure or inspection would damage the public interest.'

So the common law of public interest immunity, and its statutory embodiments, are unaffected by the Part.

Chapter 5
The European Dimension

5.	**Introduction**
5.1	It is symbolic (some would say symptomatic) of the direction in which UK law is heading that the two most important recent statutes which have an impact on the law of confidentiality are genuinely European in origin. One important effect of this increasing homogenisation of law across Europe will be that UK lawyers will need to spend more time considering the case law of their continental brethren.
5.2	This Chapter deals with two important UK Acts of Parliament, both introduced to enact important European legislation: (i) the Data Protection Act 1998, which was designed to put into effect the European Directive on the protection of individuals with regard to the processing of personal data and on the free movement of such data[68] ('the Data Protection Directive'); (ii) the Human Rights Act 1998, which incorporates into UK law the European Convention for the Protection of Human Rights and Fundamental Freedoms[69] and certain of the protocols thereto ('the Convention').
5.3	**The Data Protection Act 1998**
5.3.1	This Act supersedes and repeals the Data Protection Act 1984. It is much stricter and encompasses many more users of data than the old legislation. It was

---

68 (1995 OJ L 281).
69 (Rome, 4 November 1950; TS 71 (1953); Cmnd 8969).

enacted to put into effect the Data Protection Directive. It applies to computerised and manual data. The Act came into force on 1 March 2000.

5.3.2   The Act regulates the processing and use of all data (including information held in manual filing systems). The Act creates two relevant categories of person: (i) a data subject;[70] (ii) a data controller.[71] A data subject is an individual who is the subject of personal data (as to which, see below). A patient will plainly be a data subject for the purposes of the Act. A data controller is a person who determines the purposes for which and the manner in which any personal data are, or are to be, processed. In the clinical field, the NHS Trust or Health Authority will be a data controller (nominating a representative). It is possible that an individual doctor will be a data controller. Each individual general practitioner will be a data controller.

5.3.3   A data controller must notify and register with the newly created Data Protection Commissioner, who will maintain a register.[72] Personal data must not be processed unless the data controller has notified the Commissioner.[73] Processing information without registration is a criminal offence, punishable by a fine. A data controller may employ a data processor to process information on his behalf.[74]

5.3.4   The Act defines what is meant by 'data' and 'personal data' (data which can lead to the identification of a living individual).[75] Of particular importance in the clinical field is the further sub-category of 'sensitive personal data', which includes 'information as to ... [the] physical or mental health and condition [of the data subject].'[76]

---

70 Section 1(1).
71 *ibid*.
72 Section 18.
73 Section 17.
74 Section 1(1).
75 Section 1(1).
76 Section 2(e).

5.3.5   The Act regulates the processing (which includes, eg organising, consulting, using, disclosing, destroying) of data. Personal data and sensitive personal data are only to be processed in accordance with the 'data protection principles'.[77] The most important are: (i) the first principle: personal data may only be processed fairly and lawfully; (ii) the third principle: personal data shall be adequate, relevant and not excessive: (iii) the fourth principle: personal data shall be accurate and kept up to date; (iv) the fifth principle: personal data shall not be kept for any longer than necessary for the purpose for which they were processed; (v) the seventh principle: adequate technical and organisational measures shall be taken to prevent unauthorised or unlawful processing of such data, and against loss, destruction or damage; (vi) the eighth principle: personal data may not be transferred outside the European Economic Area unless the recipient country or territory has adequate levels of protection for the rights and freedoms of data subjects.

5.3.6   Note that, because of the wide definitions of 'processing' and 'data', oral disclosure of health records or the information which forms the basis of those health records (whether by transmission, dissemination or otherwise making available) will be caught by the provisions of the Act. The repercussions of this remain to be seen but may well have a huge impact on the law of confidentiality.

5.3.7   Detailed guidance is given in the Act to the interpretation of each of the data protection principles.[78] These include: (i) as to the first principle, data are to be treated as fairly obtained if obtained from a person who is authorised by any enactment to supply it or who is required to supply it by any enactment, convention or other instrument imposing an international obligation on the UK; (ii) as to the seventh principle, the level of security must be appropriate to the harm which might

---

77   Section 4 and Schedule 1 part I.
78   Schedule 1 part II.

result from unauthorised or unlawful processing or loss destruction or damage; the data controller must take reasonable steps to ensure the reliability of his employees; data processors who process data on behalf of a data controller must do so under a written contract which requires them to comply with the seventh data protection principle.

5.3.8   Doctor users of email and the Internet should note that concern has been expressed about GPnet, the scheme to link family doctors to NHSnet; it has been suggested that it is neither secure nor reliable. NHSnet is currently under review and security systems such as data encryption are necessary in order to carry patient data on the network. This has particular relevance to the seventh data protection principle above.

5.3.9   Further schedules set out the circumstances which must exist before personal data (schedule 2) and sensitive personal data (schedule 3) can be processed. Of particular importance in the clinical field is that, before sensitive personal data can be processed, at least one of the conditions in schedule 3 must be satisfied: these include: (i) the 'explicit consent' of the data subject; (ii) that such processing is necessary to protect the vital interests of the data subject where the subject cannot give consent or the data controller cannot reasonably be expected to obtain consent; (iii) the information has been made public as a result of steps deliberately taken by the data subject; (iv) the processing is necessary for the purposes of legal proceedings, legal advice or otherwise for establishing or defending legal rights; (v) the processing is necessary for medical purposes (so defined as to include: preventative medicine, medical diagnosis, medical research, the provision of care and treatment and the management of healthcare services) and is undertaken by a health professional or a person who owes a duty of confidence equivalent to that which would arise if that person were a health professional; (vi) that the data consists of information as to racial and ethnic origin and is necessary to identify and keep under review the existence or absence of equality of opportunity or treatment between persons of different racial or ethnic origin.

5.3.10   A 'health professional'[79] is defined to include: (i) a registered medical practitioner; (ii) a registered dentist; (iii) a registered optician; (iv) a registered pharmaceutical chemist; (v) a registered nurse, midwife or health visitor; (vi) a registered osteopath; (vii) a registered chiropractor; (viii) a clinical psychologist, child psychotherapist or speech therapist.

5.3.11   As well as regulating the processing of data, the Act provides for: (i) a right of access to personal data by the data subject[80] (see too Chapter 6 of this book); (ii) a right to prevent processing personal data which is likely to cause damage or distress;[81] (iii) a right to prevent the processing of personal data for the purposes of direct marketing;[82] (iv) certain rights in relation to automated decision-taking.[83] Any individual who suffers damage or distress by reason of any contravention by a data controller of any of the requirements of the Act is entitled to compensation for that damage and/or distress.[84] It is a defence for the data controller to show that he took such care as was in all the circumstances reasonable to comply with the requirement concerned.[85] The High Court or a county court may, if satisfied on the application of a data subject that personal data are inaccurate, order the rectification, blocking, erasure or destruction of those data.[86]

5.3.12   If the Commissioner is satisfied that a data controller has contravened or is contravening any of the data protection principles, she may serve an enforcement

---

79 Section 69.
80 Section 7.
81 Section 10.
82 Section 11.
83 Section 12.
84 Section 13.
85 *ibid.*
86 Section 14.

notice requiring the data controller to comply with the relevant principle within a specified time or to refrain from processing any personal data after such time as may be specified[87]. A data subject may ask the Commissioner for an assessment as to whether any data processing is being carried out in accordance with, or in contravention of, the data protection principles[88]. On receipt of such a request, the Commissioner may serve an information notice on the data controller, requiring certain information to be provided within a specified time[89]. Failure to comply with an enforcement notice or an information notice (including knowingly or recklessly making a false statement in purported compliance) is a criminal offence[90], punishable by a fine.

5.3.13   It is only possible to give the briefest of overviews in this Chapter. Further information (including guidance from the Commissioner) can be obtained on the Data Protection website at: http://www.dataprotection.gov.uk/

5.3.14   The Data Protection Commissioner will not wish to become too attached to her title, for it is due to change when the Freedom of Information Bill (before the House of Lords at the time of writing) becomes law, when she will become the Information Commissioner. To what extent the Bill will affect health records is at present speculative, although information held by Health Authorities and NHS Trusts will in principle be subject to disclosure. At present it is likely that the list of exempt categories of information will emasculate the otherwise worthy principles propounded in the Bill. The right of access of a data subject to his or her health records is dealt with elsewhere.

5.3.15   **Lessons:**
           • *Ensure that you have notified the Data Protection Commissioner as a data controller.*
           • *Familiarise yourself with the data protection principles.*

---

87 Section 40.
88 Section 42.
89 Section 43.
90 Section 47.

5.4	**The Human Rights Act 1998**
5.4.1	**Introduction**

The European Convention on Human Rights and Fundamental Freedoms was ratified by the British government on 8 March 1951 and came into force on 23 September 1953. Until the passing of HRA 1998, there was no right of individual petition, nor would the UK accept the European Court of Human Rights' jurisdiction in individual cases. To date there have been well over 50 judgments in UK cases in the E Ct HR finding, many receiving substantial coverage in the national media, breaches of Convention rights. The passing of the Human Rights Act 1998 ('HRA 1998') represents the culmination of political pressure (first voiced publicly in 1968) for the incorporation of Convention rights by statute. HRA 1998 comes into force on 1 October 2000.

5.4.2   **What the Act says**

5.4.2.1   HRA 1998 s1 provides that certain Convention rights (Articles 2-12 and 14 of the Convention, Articles 1-3 of the first protocol and articles 1 and 2 of the sixth protocol, in each case read with Articles 16-18 of the Convention) are to be given (further) effect in domestic law.

5.4.2.2   HRA 1998 s2 requires UK courts and tribunals to take account of the judgments, decisions, declarations, etc, of the E Ct HR, the Commission, etc, so far as is relevant to the proceedings (see below on Interpretation). UK courts are not, however, bound to follow such judgments, etc.

5.4.2.3   HRA 1998 s3 requires primary and subordinate legislation to be read and given effect in a way which is compatible with the Convention, wherever possible.

5.4.2.4   HRA 1998 s4 enables specified courts (higher courts) to make a declaration of incompatibility, where it is satisfied that legislation is incompatible with a Convention right.

5.4.2.5   HRA 1998 s5 entitles the Crown to intervene where a court is considering making a s4 declaration.

5.4.2.6   HRA 1998 s6 makes it unlawful for a public authority to act in a way which is incompatible with a Convention right. It is an exception if (i) the public authority, as a result of primary legislation, could not have acted differently or; (ii) the public authority was giving effect to provisions of or under primary legislation. An act includes a failure to act.

5.4.2.7   A public authority includes a court or tribunal. It also includes any person some of whose functions are functions of a public nature, though a person is not a public authority if the nature of the act is private. Persons or organisations who may be challenged include: central government (excluding executive agencies), local government, the police, immigration officers, prisons, NHS trusts and health authorities.

5.4.2.8   HRA 1998 s7 identifies how a person may bring a claim against, before a domestic court or tribunal, a public authority alleged to be in breach of HRA s6. Such a person may bring proceedings in the appropriate court or tribunal or may rely on the Convention right(s) in any legal proceedings but must be a victim of the unlawful act. To be a victim, a person must be a victim for the purposes of Article 34 of the Convention (see below).

5.4.2.9   HRA 1998 s8 enables a court or tribunal to grant remedies where a public authority has (or proposes to act) in breach of a Convention right. A court or tribunal may in those circumstances grant such relief as it considers just and appropriate. Damages may only be awarded by a court or tribunal which has power to award damages (ie civil courts only) and only if necessary to afford just satisfaction to the victim. There is no 'right' to compensation as such.

5.4.2.10   HRA 1998 s9 allows decisions of courts or tribunals to be challenged only by way of appeal (save where judicial review is available). Damages cannot be awarded in respect of a judicial act done in good faith (other than to compensate to the extent required by

Article 5(5) of the Convention (arrest or detention in contravention of the Convention).

5.4.2.11   HRA 1998 s10 enables speedy amendments to provisions which have been declared to be incompatible with the Convention by a court pursuant to s4.

5.4.2.12   HRA 1998 s12 ensures that courts will pay particular regard to the right to freedom of expression.

5.4.2.13   HRA 1998 s13 ensures that courts will pay particular regard to the right to freedom of thought, conscience and religion as exercised by religious organisations and their members.

5.4.3   **Interpretation**

5.4.3.1   The Convention is a living, breathing entity, which is capable of dynamic and creative interpretation and development: 'a living instrument which ... must be interpreted in the light of present-day conditions'.[91] Where social mores change, so interpretation of Convention rights is capable of change. The Convention is supposed to guarantee practical and effective rights, not abstruse theoretical ones. It should ensure balance between the individual and the community. In particular the doctrine of proportionality requires that a restriction on any particular freedom guaranteed under the Convention must be 'proportionate to the legitimate aim pursued'.[92] Accordingly, construing a Convention Article is not like construing a UK statute, but rather requires flexibility and latitude.

5.4.3.2   The doctrine of 'margin of appreciation' is particularly important. 'By reason of their direct and continuous contact with the vital forces of their countries, the national authorities are in principle better placed than an international court to evaluate local needs and conditions'.[93] Technically the doctrine will not apply to consideration of the Convention by domestic courts, but there may be circumstances where the court or

---

91 Application 5856/72, *Tyrer v UK* (1978) 2 EHRR 1.
92 Application 5493/72, *Handyside v UK* (1976) 1 EHRR 737, 754 (para 49).
93 Application 20348/92, *Buckley v UK* (1996) 23 EHRR 101, 129 (para 75).

tribunal will consider that the legislature and executive are better placed to balance the competing needs referred to above and will accordingly defer to the executive. Concern has been expressed about the possible conflation of this principle with the *Wednesbury unreasonableness* doctrine.

5.5   **European Convention on Human Rights**

5.5.1   Without doubt, the most significant Article affecting the area of clinical confidentiality is Article 8:

Article 8 – Right to respect for private and family life, home and correspondence

1.   Everyone has the right to respect for his private and family life, his home and his correspondence.

2.   There shall be no interference by a public authority with the exercise of this right except such as is in accordance with the law and is necessary in a democratic society in the interests of national security, public safety or the economic well-being of the country, for the prevention of disorder or crime, for the protection of health or morals, or for the protection of the rights and freedoms of others.

5.5.2   Unlike certain other Convention rights (eg Article 2 (right to life), Article 3 (freedom from inhuman or degrading treatment or punishment), which are absolute, this is a qualified right. Its impact on English law may nonetheless be considerable. It is much broader than a protection of privacy alone. It includes the right to keep to oneself. The European Court has affirmed the importance of preserving the confidentiality of medical records.[94]

5.5.3   The collection of medical data and the maintenance of medical records is likely to be affected by Article 8. In *MS v Sweden*[95] the applicant had made a claim for compensation from the Social Insurance Office arising from a back injury at work. The Office requested her

---

94 *Z v Finland*, (1998) 25 EHRR 371.
95 (1999) 28 EHRR 313.

medical records (without her consent) from the head of the clinic who had treated her for a longstanding back condition. The records suggested that an abortion had been performed due to the back condition, making no reference to the accident at work (the abortion being four years later than the accident) and the Office rejected the claim. The Court held that there had been an interference with her right under Article 8 but that the interference was justified since it served the legitimate aim of protection of the economic well-being of the country. Importantly, the Court indicated that the applicant had not waived her right to respect for her private life by submitting a claim for compensation. The ramifications of this are potentially enormous.

5.5.4   The European Court and Commission have considered Article 8 in the context of: (i) disclosure, compulsory in Swedish law, by a psychiatrist of an applicant's medical condition where that might have affected the welfare of her child (no breach of Article 8);[96] (ii) refusal by the UK to amend its system of registering births so as to permit post-operative transsexuals to record their new sexual identity (no breach);[97] (iii) failure by the UK to disclose medical records to alleged victims of nuclear weapons testing in the 1950s (no breach);[98] (iv) disclosure of identity of AIDS sufferer in course of judgment by Supreme Court of Finland and order to make medical records public after 2002 (breach of Article 8);[99] (v) orders requiring doctors to give evidence as to awareness of HIV/AIDS status against patient during criminal trial (no breach).[100]

---

96 *Andersson v Sweden*, (1998) 25 EHRR 722.
97 *Sheffield v UK*, (1999) 27 EHRR 163.
98 *McGinley v UK*, (1999) 27 EHRR 1.
99 *Z v Finland*, (1998) 25 EHRR 371.
100 *ibid*.

5.5.5   *MS v Sweden* 23 EHRR 313, European Court of Human
Rights
**Confidentiality; Article 8 of European Convention on
Human Rights**
The applicant was a Swedish citizen who was previously employed as a nursery school teacher. She suffered from a pre-existing condition of the spine which can cause chronic back pain. In October 1991 she slipped and fell at work, injuring her back. As she was pregnant at the time, she visited her doctor at the women's clinic. Following her accident, she was unable to resume work on a regular basis and was in due course granted a disability pension. She made a claim for compensation under the Industrial Injury Insurance Act from the Social Security Office ('SSO'). She then discovered that, in response to a request for her medical records during the relevant period by the SSO, and without consulting her, the women's clinic had supplied copies of records from up to five years following the accident. These included details of an abortion she had had as a result of her pre-existing back condition. Her claim for compensation was rejected on the basis that her sick leave had not been caused by industrial injury. Her subsequent appeals were all dismissed. She argued before the European Court that the submission of her records to the SSO constituted an unjustified interference with her right to respect for private life under Article 8.

The Court held that there had been no breach of Article 8. In particular the Court noted that her medical data were passed from one public institution to another in the context of an assessment of whether she satisfied the legal conditions for obtaining a benefit which she herself had requested. The SSO had a legitimate need to check information received from her against data in possession of the clinic. Accordingly there were relevant and sufficient reasons for the communication of her medical records by the clinic to the SSO.

5.5.6   *Z v Finland* 25 EHRR 371; European Court of Human Rights

Confidentiality; Article 8 of European Convention on Human Rights

The applicant was a Swedish national married to X, whom she had met in Africa. During an investigation of X for a number of sexual offences, it was discovered that he was HIV positive. He was tried on several counts of attempted manslaughter of women with whom he had had sexual intercourse. As it was not clear that he had knowledge of his condition at the time of commission of all the sexual assaults, the issue at trial was when he obtained such knowledge. In an attempt to discover this (and because Z had invoked her legal right not to give evidence), orders were issued obliging the medical advisers treating both X and Z to give evidence. The police also seized medical records belonging to Z. X was convicted on several counts of attempted manslaughter. The Court of Appeal disclosed both the applicant's identity and her medical data in the course of judgment. The local courts ruled that confidentiality should be maintained for ten years. The applicant complained that there had been violations to her right to respect for private and family life under Article 8, invoking: (i) the orders requiring her medical advisers to give evidence; (ii) the seizure of her medical records; (iii) the decisions to limit confidentiality to ten years; (iv) the disclosure of her identity and medical data in the course of judgment.

The Court held that: (i) there was no breach of Article 8 in ordering her medical advisers to give evidence. The evidence was potentially decisive for the purpose of determining the issue at the trial of X. There were important public interest considerations in favour of investigating and prosecuting the offences; (ii) the seizure of her medical records did not breach Article 8, for similar reasons to (i) above; (iii) the order to make the transcripts of the evidence of the doctors and her medical records public in 2002 would, if implemented, constitute a breach of Article 8. All parties had requested a longer period and there was no overriding public interest consideration; (iv) the disclosure of her identity and medical condition constituted a breach of Article 8 and there were no cogent reasons for the publication.

5.5.7 *Andersson (Anne-Marie) v Sweden* 25 EHRR 722; European Court of Human Rights

Confidentiality; Article 8 of the European Convention on Human Rights

The applicant, A, a Swedish citizen living in Gothenberg, was divorced and living with her son, SA. From May 1988 onwards she suffered from the effects of severe dental problems, as a result of which she was unable to work. She also suffered from severe anxiety. In August 1991 she was warned by the chief psychiatrist about the possible detrimental effect that her condition might have on SA and advised to seek support from either the social authorities or the children's psychiatric clinic. She did not consider those steps necessary. In January 1992 the psychiatrist informed her that in view of the risk to SA's health he was obliged to inform the Swedish authorities. He did so with her knowledge but without her consent. At the request of the social authorities the psychiatrist submitted a report to them about the state of her health. SA was placed in a non-residential therapeutic school with A's agreement. In February 1992 A complained to the European Commission (formerly the screening body to the full Court) that, *inter alia*, her right to respect for private and family life under Article 8 had been breached. Following A's death, SA sought to continue the proceedings before the full court.

The Court held that in the circumstances A had no arguable claim that there had been any violation of Article 8. The measures taken pursued the legitimate aims of protecting the 'health and morals' and 'rights and freedoms of others' and was necessary in a democratic society.

5.5.8   UK courts have considered Article 8 in the context of:
(i) the closure of a nursing home for the severely disabled (potential breach of Article 8);[101] (ii) the introduction of random drug testing for prisoners (no breach);[102] (iii) a Health Authority's refusal to disclose medical records (no breach).[103]

5.5.9   The rights in Article 8 must be balanced against the rights in Article 10 (freedom of expression), again a qualified right to be balanced by the needs of a democratic society. Indeed it has been suggested by some commentators that, once the Human Rights Act 1998 takes effect and courts become more comfortable with considering human rights issues, the law of confidentiality will or may become subsumed into a more general law of privacy, balanced by a fundamental right to freedom of expression.

5.5.10   The national media have written a number of dramatically worded stories about the possible impact of the Convention. Much of them are simple scare-stories. An analysis of the reported cases shows that, while the Court has listened to some of the more unusual arguments, it has had no hesitation in throwing out those which are obvious nonsense. Moreover, articles in the press about the possible impact of the Convention express no more than what is possible: most are, frankly, unlikely. Until the Act comes into force and courts become used to dealing with Convention points of law, most of the column space devoted to the area remains firmly in the realm of speculation. For those who are worried about the impact of HRA 1998, the recent words of Buxton LJ may provide some comfort:

'In a case where neither Convention nor Community rights can be asserted, the case either succeeds or fails on domestic law grounds and on no other. And with the imminent coming into force of the Human Rights Act it will be even more important than it is at present to

---

101 *R v North & East Devon HA, ex parte Coughlan* [1999] Lloyd's Rep Med 306, CA.
102 *R v SoS for Home Department, ex parte Tremayne* unreported; QBD 2.5.96.
103 *R v Mid Glamorgan Family Health Services, ex parte Martin* [1995] 1 WLR 110, CA.

ensure that Convention rights are not asserted in inappropriate circumstances; so that they play their proper, and important role, but only their proper role, in the protection of the citizen's interests.'[104]

More recently still, the Court of Appeal emphasised in the context of the Civil Procedure Rules 1998 that it was undesirable for issues in civil proceedings to be complicated by the injection of arguments based on Article 6 of the Convention (right to a fair trial) and it hoped that judges would be robust in resisting such arguments.[105]

5.5.11   The European Court of Human Rights has a good and searchable, if sometimes extremely slow, website at http://www.echr.coe.int/

104 *North West Lancashire HA v A, D & G* [1999] Lloyd's Rep Med 399, CA.
105 *Daniels v Walker* CA; unreported; 3.5.2000.

Chapter 6
Rights of Access to Health Records Other Than in the Course of Litigation

6.1	**Introduction**
6.1.1	This chapter considers rights of access by patients to their medical records other than in the course of litigation.
6.1.2	The right of access is now seen as increasingly important if not fundamental in a society where any number of agencies (including credit reference agencies, insurance companies, etc) hold confidential information and make decisions based on that information which can have drastic effects on our lives. Some right of access for the purposes of verification and supervision is essential in a democratic society.
6.2	**The position at common law**
6.2.1	Whatever the academics say (and they say a lot), a patient has no unfettered right of access to health records at common law.[106] The Patient's Charter[107] states: 'You have the right ... to have access to your health records, and to know that everyone working for the NHS is under a legal duty to keep your records confidential.'

---

106 *R v Mid Glamorgan HSA ex parte Martin* [1995] 1 WLR 110, CA.
107 Published by the Department of Health, 1996.

6.2.2   A health authority is not entitled to make such use of any health records as it chooses. A health professional has a general duty to act in the patient's best interests and can deny a patient access to his health records if it is in his best interests to do so.[108] The NHS has issued guidance that access should usually be provided voluntarily in the interests of good medical practice.[109]

6.2.3   *R v Mid Glamorgan FHSA, ex parte Martin*
[1995] 1 WLR 110, CA
Access to medical records; non-statutory application
The applicant, who had a background of psychological problems, had from the late 1960s repeatedly requested access to his medical records in the possession of the relevant health authorities. Those records were not subject to the Access to Health Records Act 1990 nor to the Data Protection Act 1984. The health authorities refused voluntary disclosure direct to the applicant on the grounds that to do so would be detrimental to him and not in his best interests. They offered sight to his medical adviser who could determine whether access would be likely to cause harm to the applicant. In proceedings for judicial review, the first instance judge held that the applicant had no right of access to his medical records at common law and that there had been no breach of Article 8 of the European Convention on Human Rights by the health authorities. The applicant appealed.

The Court of Appeal dismissed the appeal. A health authority was bound to deal with medical records in the same way as a private doctor. A health authority could deny a patient access to his medical records if it was in the patient's best interests to do so. The authorities had complied with their duty in the action they had taken. Nourse LJ noted that a health authority had no absolute right to deal with medical records in any way it chose. It had a general duty to act in the best interests of the patient. Those interests usually required that

---

108 *Ex parte Martin [supra]*.
109 Health Service Guidance (91)6.

medical records would not be disclosed to a third party, although they would usually be handed on by one doctor to another or made available to the patient's legal advisers if reasonably required for the purposes of litigation involving the patient.

6.3   **Data Protection Act 1998**

6.3.1   Chapter 5 above contains further information about the Data Protection Act 1998 ('DPA').

6.3.2   A data subject has a general right of access to his personal data.[110] However, in the context of personal data consisting of information as to the physical or mental health or condition of the data subject, the right of access has been modified by the Data Protection (Subject Access Modification) (Health) Order 2000.[111]

6.3.3   Such personal data is exempt from the general access provisions in any case to the extent that access would be likely to cause serious harm to the physical or mental health or condition of the data subject or any other person.[112] Clinicians will be familiar with this test and it is important to note that the data controller (if he is not the treating clinician) must always seek the views of the relevant treating clinician on that point.[113] The obligation to consult does not apply where the data subject has already seen or knows about the information requested or in certain limited circumstances where consultation has been carried out prior to the request being made.[114]

6.3.4   A data controller cannot refuse access on the grounds that the identity of a third party would be disclosed in cases where the information is contained in a health record and the third party is a health professional who has compiled or contributed to that health record or has been involved in the care of data subject except in the (presumably rare) circumstances where serious

110 Section 7.
111 SI 2000/413.
112 Article 5(1).
113 Article 5(2).
114 Articles 6 and 7.

harm is likely to be caused to that health professional's physical or mental health or condition by giving access to the data subject.[115]

6.3.5   It would be nice to be able to say that the DPA provides an all-embracing and permanent system for access to health records. Not so, for the Freedom of Information Bill (before the House of Lords at the time of writing) threatens to amend the DPA almost before we had a chance to become used to it. The Bill provides a right of access to information held by public bodies (including Health Authorities and NHS Trusts.) Personal information relating to the applicant will be covered by the DPA. The disclosure of information which would endanger the physical or mental health or safety of any individual is exempt from disclosure, as is information provided in confidence. Criticism has already been made of the Bill that the list of exempt material is so wide as to emasculate the (worthy) principle of open access to information.

6.4   **Access to Medical Reports Act 1988**

6.4.1   This Act came into force on 1 January 1989. It gives patients the right to see certain medical reports prepared about them for employment or insurance purposes.

6.4.2   A medical report is defined to mean 'a report ... relating to the physical or mental health of the individual prepared by a medical practitioner who is or has been responsible for the clinical care of the individual'.[116] The supply of a report 'for insurance or employment purposes' is to be construed as a reference to 'the supply of such a report for insurance or employment purposes which are purposes of the person who is seeking to be supplied with it'. It will be seen that this definition does not cover an independent health professional who does not have and has never had a doctor-patient relationship with the person concerned.

---

115 Article 8.
116 Section 2(1).

There has been some debate about whether occupational health doctors (who are employed to advise both the employer and the employee about health and safety at work) are covered. The answer is a classic lawyer's answer: it depends in this case on the extent of the relationship between the doctor and the employee and whether the doctor has responsibility as a treating clinician for that person.

6.4.3   A person may not apply to a medical practitioner for a medical report for employment or insurance purposes unless he has told the individual concerned that he proposes to make the application and the individual has consented.[117] The individual shall be entitled to see the report before it is supplied, in which case the medical report may not be supplied before the individual has had the chance to request any amendments nor without the individual's consent.[118] Individuals should not be deflected by the insistence of insurance salesmen that supply of reports in advance takes too much time as the right is fundamental.

6.4.4   A medical practitioner may refuse access to the report where: (i) disclosure would be likely to cause serious harm to the individual or others or would 'indicate the intentions of the practitioner in respect of the individual' (whatever that means);[119] (ii) disclosure would reveal the identity of a third party unless that person has not consented or is a health professional involved in the care of the individual.[120] The doctor must advise the individual that his application is refused under one of the exceptions above.

6.4.5   The county court has jurisdiction to hear applications where an individual seeks and has been refused access and can order disclosure.[121]

---

117 Section 4.
118 Section 5.
119 Section 7(1).
120 Section 7(2).
121 Section 8.

6.5   **Access to Health Records Act 1990**

6.5.1   Since the coming into force of the Data Protection Act 1998 and the Data Protection (Subject Access Modification) (Health) Order 2000 (as to which, see above), the Access to Health Records Act 1990 has lost most of its significance. This is because it was originally passed to cover certain manual health records, which were not covered by the Data Protection Act 1984. Now the Data Protection Act 1998 covers manual as well as computer-held documents.

6.5.2   In its amended form the Access to Health Records Act 1990 enables an application for health records to be made only where a patient has died, either by the personal representative of the patient or by any person who may have a claim arising out of the patient's death.[122]

6.6   **Access to health records by a third party**

6.6.1   It is possible to imagine circumstances in which it is not the patient who wishes to have access to his records, but some other person (eg the parents of a child or a patient's spouse). Such a request may be made because the patient is unable to consent to disclosure or to understand the health records if they were disclosed. The position may be acute where a relative is concerned that the clinicians may not be offering appropriate treatment.

6.6.2   The Data Protection Act 1998 gives no right to access to anyone other than a data subject. Requests for access must therefore be made on non-statutory grounds.

6.6.3   In particular the General Medical Council's guidance to doctors set out in its booklet 'Confidentiality'[123] states: '2. You may release confidential information in strict accordance with the patient's consent, or the consent of a person properly authorised to act on the patient's behalf.' Patients who are competent to do so

---

122 Section 3, as amended by the Data Protection Act 1998 schedule 16 Part 1.
123 October 1995 (with some additions in 1996). See also the GMC booklet 'Serious Communicable Diseases' October 1997: (Both are at Appendix 1 below).

may wish to draft some form of consent to the disclosure of health records to a named individual or individuals.

Chapter 7
Remedies for Breach of Confidence

7.1   Introduction

7.1.1   This chapter is concerned with remedies for breach of confidence in civil actions for breach of confidence. It does not deal with situations where statute imposes penalties for breaches of confidence. Those situations are dealt with in Chapter 3.

7.1.2   A number of remedies are available in breach of confidence actions. They include injunctions, orders for destruction or delivery up of the relevant documents, accounts of profits, declarations of constructive trusts, other declarations, and awards of damages.

7.2.   Injunctions

7.2.1   Usually what a person whose confidence has been breached wants most is an order restraining further breaches of that confidence.

7.2.2   Interim injunctions, pending final determination of the issues, are very commonly granted, and often have to be applied for very quickly.

7.2.3   The principles governing the grant of interim injunctions are set out in *American Cyanamid v Ethicon*.[124] The court will consider:

---

124 [1975] AC 396.

- *Whether or not there is a serious issue to be tried*

The claim must not be frivolous or vexatious, and must have some prospect of success.[125] But an application for an interim injunction is not a place to resolve conflicts of fact or difficult issues of law.

- *Where the balance of convenience lies*

Here, the courts have prescribed a rigid structure of questions:

(a)   Are damages an adequate remedy for the claimant? Is the defendant able to pay damages? If the answer to both questions is yes, there will be no injunction. If no, go on to ask ...

(b)   Is the undertaking as to damages which the claimant will have to give sufficient protection for the defendant? If yes, the injunction will be granted. If no, go on to consider ...

(c)   The maintenance of the status quo ante. The court will normally think it best for the status quo prior to the alleged breach to be maintained insofar as an injunction can achieve that. Also consider:

(d)   Other factors, including social and economic ones, the public interest, and (as a last resort – really scraping the bottom of the forensic barrel), the relative strength of the parties' cases.

7.2.4   There are exceptions to the *American Cyanamid* principles, notably where the grant of an interim injunction will effectively dispose of the whole case. But these exceptions are not very important in the context of clinical confidentiality disputes.

7.2.5   Probably, once a confidence has been breached, an injunction cannot be granted preventing making otherwise lawful profits using the confidential information.[126]

7.2.6   When applying for an interim injunction, take tremendous care to specify exactly what it should attach to. If

---

125 *Re Cable* [1975] 1 WLR 7; *Smith v ILEA* [1978] 1 All ER 411.

126 In *Kaye v Robertson* [1991] FSR 62 a journalist had unlawfully taken pictures, but no injunction was available to stop him profiting from their publication.

the order is granted in terms so wide that disclosure of some non-confidential material is prevented, the undertaking in damages might bite,[127] (although in practice in clinical confidentiality the undertaking in damages is likely to be pretty toothless.

7.2.7   The principles on which permanent injunctions are granted are the normal equitable ones. Injunctions will not be granted where damages will be sufficient, they will not be granted to people without equitably clean hands, and they will not be granted to restrain something which does not need restraining. For this last reason (because the courts are reluctant to conclude that the disclosure of most kinds of information will *always* need restraining) perpetual injunctions are hard to come by.

7.2.8   The procedure for applying for interim injunctions is set out in CPR Part 25 and 25 CPD.

7.3.   **Account of profits**

7.3.1   Equity has long ordered persons who benefit from their breach of confidence to account to a claimant for that profit. The exact nature of the remedy is controversial. Thus although the traditional justification for the power to order an account has been that no one should be allowed to gain from his own wrongdoing,[128] and that equity must therefore have a power which prevents such unlawful gain, it may be better to analyse the remedy as restitution.[129] For practical purposes it makes no difference. The claimant will be able to claw back monies generated by reason of the breach.

7.3.2   Damages and an account are alternatives.[130] Otherwise there would be double recovery. But an account can be obtained along with other remedies.[131]

---

127 See, for instance: *Universal Thermosensor Ltd v Hibben* [1992] 1 WLR 840 and, more generally, *Times Newspapers Ltd v MGN Ltd* [1993] EMLR 442.
128 See, for instance, the *Spycatcher* case, [1990] 1 AC 109, per Lord Keith at 262.
129 Per Lord Goff in *Spycatcher* at 286.
130 *Sutherland Publishing Co Ltd v Caxton Publishing Co Ltd* [1936] Ch 323.
131 *Peter Pan Manufacturing Corporation v Corsets Silhouette Ltd* [1964] 1 WLR 96.

7.4   **Constructive trusts**

7.4.1   Constructive trusts show the courts at their most prag-
           matic and creative. If, for instance, information
           obtained in breach of a fiduciary duty allows a defen-
           dant to obtain some sort of financial gain, the court
           may hold that the defendant holds the property as a
           constructive trustee for the person whose confidence
           has been breached.[132] Probably the courts in the future
           will be ready to imply fiduciary responsibility into
           patient-doctor relationships.

7.5.   **Orders for delivery up or destruction**

7.5.1   There is nothing conceptually or practically difficult
           about this. If the defendant holds confidential informa-
           tion which he should not have, the court can compel
           him to hand it over or destroy it.[133]

7.5.2   The remedy of course is discretionary, and the court
           applies the maxims of equity in deciding whether to
           exercise the discretion. Thus if the documents con-
           cerned do not exist, the court, which does not like to act
           in vain, is unlikely to make an order of this type. If
           damages can properly compensate, the order is likely
           to be for damages instead.[134]

7.6.   **Damages**

7.6.1   Damages are available in common law for:
           (a) breach of a duty of confidence owed under a con-
                tract; and
           (b) inducement of such a breach of contract.

7.6.2   Damages are available in lieu of an injunction under
           s50 of the Supreme Court Act 1981.

7.6.3   This raises the obvious point: what if there has been a
           non-contractual breach of confidence for which an
           injunction is, for whatever reason, not available?
           Sir Robert Megarry V-C, in *Malone v Metropolitan Police*

---

132 See *Phipps v Boardman* [1967] 2 AC 46.
133 See, for example, *Robb v Green* [1895] 2 QB 315; *Prince Albert v Strange* (1849) 2
    De G & SM 652.
134 See, for instance, *Saltman* (1948) 65 RPC 203.

Commissioner,[135] thought it doubtful whether, in these circumstances, damages, as opposed to an account of profits, were available.

7.6.4 But nonetheless a number of commentators, supported by dicta in the House of Lords, have suggested that equitable damages can be awarded generally for breach of an equitable duty of confidence.[136]

7.6.5 The quantification of financial loss in breach of confidence cases is easy in theory, if not in practice. But the recoverability of damages for distress as a result of the breach of confidence is highly controversial.

7.6.6 In tort, damages cannot be obtained for any sort of distress or shaking up which does not amount to a recognisable psychiatric injury.[137]

7.6.7 In contract, damages generally cannot be obtained for distress even where it is reasonably foreseeable that distress will result from a breach of contract,[138] unless it is possible to construe the contract as a contract to provide peace of mind[139] or some other positive benefit.[140] In such cases the damages are best construed as awards for the absence of the benefit contracted for, not as awards compensating for the detriment of the distress.

7.6.8 Of course actions for breach of confidence are legally curious. They might arise out of a breach of contract, or they may not. Even when they spring from contractual loins they are still to some extent equitable animals. But is that a reason to say that they should not be ruled by the ordinary rules governing recoverability of damages? If non-contractual breach of confidence cases are to have special rules, contractual breach of

135 [1979] 1 Ch 344, at p360.
136 See Toulson and Phipps, *Confidentiality*, 1996: para 10.10. Also *United Scientific Holdings Ltd v Burnley Borough Council* [1978] AC 904.
137 See, for example, *Nicholls v Rushton*, The Times, 19 June 1992. There are exceptions: defamation is the obvious one.
138 See, for example, *Addis v Gramophone Co*, [1909] AC 488, and *Hayes v Dodd* [1990] 2 All ER 815.
139 As in *Heywood v Wellers* [1976] QB 446.
140 As in the spoilt holiday cases, such as *Jarvis v Swan Tours Ltd* [1973] QB 233.

confidences cases should have them too: it would be bizarrely anomalous were a party in a contractual relationship to be entitled to less compensation than someone without the protection of contract. Strangely, it has not yet been decided in England whether or not the *sui generis* character of breach of confidence actions entitles the courts to depart from the usual rules about recoverability of damages for distress. It is suggested that the courts should be allowed to compensate for distress. Breaches of confidence will very commonly produce tremendous distress. There are often no foreseeability problems at all. The essence of the action is that that foreseeable distress has been caused by unconscionable conduct on the part of the defendant. Commonly, too, there will be no demonstrable pecuniary loss. It would be unfair if the defendant were to get away with a mere injunction being slapped on him. The analogy with defamation is a good one.

7.6.9   If the courts are not prepared to create a separate category of recoverable damages for distress in breach of confidence cases there are ways in which the existing law could be made, with little fundamental damage, to accommodate such damages. The obligation to keep confidences could simply be construed, by analogy with the contractual duty in *Heywood v Wellers*[141] type cases, as an obligation with the purpose, inter alia, of ensuring the peace of mind of knowing that the obligation will not be broken. After all, the main thing that confiders want is that peace of mind: it is precisely to protect it that the duty is imposed on the confidee. It would be curious if no damages representing the inevitable distress which results from the breach were available.[142]

7.6.10   Exemplary damages are sometimes recoverable in clinical confidentiality cases. The principles are set out in *Rookes v Barnard*.[143] Such damages may be awarded:

---

141 Supra.
142 In *Cornelius v Dr Taranto*, unreported, 30 June 2000, Morland J held that modest damages were recoverable for injury to feelings caused by unauthorised disclosure of a medico-legal report, and also for the expenses incurred in trying to retrieve copies of the report. See too para 6.11 below.
143 [1964] AC 1129.

(a) In cases of oppressive, arbitrary or unconstitutional acts by government servants (which in some circumstances might include unwarranted disclosure of confidential information); and

(b) where the defendant's conduct had been calculated by him to make a profit which would exceed the compensation payable to the claimant (for instance by selling confidential information); and

(c) where statute expressly authorised it (for example where there has been an infringement of copyright, and s97(2) of the Copyright, Designs and Patents Act 1988 applies).[144]

7.6.11   In the limited circumstances in which exemplary damages are recoverable, the uplift on the ordinary compensatory element of damages can be regarded as being in part compensatory of the injured feelings of the claimant.[145] The injured feelings of the claimant which are being compensated for in these circumstances are not, presumably, those injured by the breach of confidence per se, but those injured by the fact of the oppressive behaviour, or the profit-making, or whatever other *Rookes v Barnard* criterion applies.

7.7.   Declarations

7.7.1   Declarations, which the court has a discretionary power to give, are often a useful way of clearing up doubts about confidentiality. Anyone, claimant, potential claimant, defendant, or potential defendant, can theoretically apply for judicial clarification.[146] Declarations can be a useful way of finding out in advance of proposed disclosure what the legal effect of the disclosure will be.

7.8.   Norwich Pharmacal orders

7.8.1   Sometimes a confidence will be breached, but the would-be claimant does not know who breached it.

---

144 See *Williams v Settle* [1960] 1 WLR 1072.
145 See *Broome v Cassell & Co* [1972] AC 1027 and *Appleton v Garrett* [1997] 8 Med LR 75.
146 See, for instance, *Price Waterhouse v BCCI Holdings (Luxembourg) SA* [1992] BCLC 583.

This is unusual in medical cases, because usually the custodian of the relevant information is well known, and even if the individual who leaked the confidence cannot be identified, the identity is an irrelevance for the purpose of proceedings, because the primary custodian will be liable. But occasionally it will be necessary to trace the leaker – for instance if medical records have been physically removed from a hospital, shown to the press, and then not returned – so that an injunction to restrain further publication can be obtained.

7.8.2   In these circumstances an action for an order forcing the recipient of the information to disclose the source of the information can be brought. These orders are called *Norwich Pharmacal* orders.[147] The principles are set out in Norwich Pharmacal itself and *British Steel Corporation v Granada Television Ltd*.[148] Detailed consideration of actions for discovery is outside the scope of this book.

---

147 From *Norwich Pharmacal Co v Customs and Excise Commissioners* [1974] AC 133.
148 [1981] AC 1096.

Chapter 8
Precedents

8.1   **Letter of claim in a breach of clinical confidentiality case**

Cry, Woolf & Co,
High St,
Thatsit,
Deathshire

The Deathshire Hospital NIIS Trust,
End Road,
Thatsit,
Deathshire

14 April 2000

Dear Sir,

Re our client Mrs Viola Ted, dob 3.4.1967

We have been consulted this morning by the above. She was referred by her general practitioner to the Deathshire District Hospital ('the hospital') for investigation of infertility, and on 1 April 2000 was seen in the out-patient clinic by a Consultant Obstetrician and Gynaecologist, Mr Ian Discreet.

In the course of our client's consultation with Mr Ian Discreet she told him that she was worried that she may have contracted syphilis in the course of an extra-marital affair. Mr Ian Discreet made no comment about this at this stage, but took swabs and blood samples which eventually confirmed that she did indeed suffer from syphilis. The diagnosis was communicated to our client at a further out-patient clinic at the hospital on 10 April 2000. Antibiotic treatment for the syphilis was then started.

On 14 April 2000 our client was visited by Ms Kidgrab, a representative from the Child Protection Unit of Deathshire Social Services. Ms Kidgrab explained that she had, that morning, received a letter from Mr Ian Discreet, telling her about our client's diagnosis of syphilis and advising the Deathshire Social Services:

(a) to tell our client to tell her husband about the diagnosis so that he could be screened for syphilis and treated if necessary; and

(b) if our client failed to communicate the diagnosis to her husband, to take steps to tell him directly; and

(c) to arrange for our client's children to be taken into care, because the circumstances in which the infection was acquired indicated that she was not fit to be a mother.

Our client, understandably, was most upset. She ordered Ms Kidgrab out of the house, and contacted us directly.

The information about the extra-marital affair and our client's concerns about syphilis were communicated to Mr Ian Discreet in circumstances of confidentiality. He undoubtedly owed her a duty to keep the information confidential. His communication of that information to Deathshire Social Services amounts to a breach of that duty. Our client has suffered great mental anguish as a result. She fears that if her husband is told about the extra-marital affair he will leave her. She fears that she will lose her children. She has totally lost confidence in the medical profession. She fears that there will be further breaches of confidence. Further we believe that the disclosure constitutes a breach of the Data Protection Act 1998, comprising as it does the disclosure of information forming part of a health record.

Given the real possibility of further imminent breaches of confidence, we can see no alternative but to protect our client's position by applying immediately for an interim injunction restraining further disclosure. We have accordingly instructed Counsel to seek such an order, and Counsel is indeed at court for that application as this letter is being dictated. We will of course serve you with the order as soon as it is made, but in the meantime we advise you to take urgent steps to prevent any further dissemination of the confidential information.

You should also take this letter as an indication that we are instructed, unless you agree now to pay substantial damages and to enter into a permanent formal undertaking not to disseminate further any confidential information provided to the hospital by our client, to issue proceedings:

(a)   for damages for breach of confidence; and

(b)   for a permanent injunction restraining further breaches of confidence.

We advise you to pass this letter on immediately to your legal advisers, and look forward to hearing from you urgently.

8.2   **The Defendant's letter of response**

Messrs Offhook,
Swishpad Lane,
Hugefees,
London SW1

Cry, Woolf & Co,
High Street,
Thatsit,
Deathshire

14 April 2000

Dear Sir,

Re Your client Mrs Viola Ted, dob 3.4.1967
Our client, the Deathshire NHS Trust

Our above named client has passed us your faxed letter of today's date. The Trust has had an opportunity to take brief instructions from Mr Ian Discreet and other staff who were present at the consultation on 1 and 10 April 2000. Such instructions as we have indicate that your client has not told you the full story, and that any attempt to seek an injunction or damages will be radically misconceived.

Your client attended the consultation on 1 April 2000 drunk. She sat in the waiting room of the hospital shouting loudly to the crowd of patients there: 'I've got syphilis, and I don't care who knows it. I got it from Ian Pus, and it was worth every penny.' A number of patients were alarmed and offended by this behaviour.

You will of course recognise the legal significance of this. The information about the syphilis is not confidential information. Your client broadcast it. Indeed she expressly disclaimed, by her words: 'I don't care who knows it', any right which she might otherwise have in relation to further disclosure of the information.

In the consultation with Mr Ian Discreet on 1 April she reiterated to him what she had been saying in the waiting room. He was therefore under no obligation of confidence in relation to the information about the infection with syphilis. She further told Mr Ian Discreet that she disliked her husband, and that although she had not had sexual intercourse with him since her affair with Ian Pus, she intended to resume sexual relations imminently with the express purpose of infecting him with syphilis.

In the course of the consultation Mr Ian Discreet noted a number of suppurating syphilitic sores on your client's hands. They led him to be very concerned about the possibility of your client's children becoming infected too.

Accordingly, even in the unlikely event of a court concluding that the information about the syphilis remained in any sense confidential, we are confident that an action for breach of confidence would fail on the grounds that the public interest in disclosure of the information outweighed the public interest in maintaining confidentiality. We respectfully, and no doubt unnecessarily, refer you to *W v Egdell* [1990] 2 WLR 471.

An action for breach of confidence would be bound to fail for other reasons, too. Even if the information about the syphilis was legally confidential at the time that it was communicated to Mr Ian Discreet, your client's treatment of that information (as evidenced by her behaviour in the waiting room) was such that your client's husband would have been bound to hear the information by some route or other no later than the time that he may now be told it by the social services. Accordingly there is no detriment. Further, if your client's children are taken into care, this will not primarily be because of the syphilitic sores. All of the healthcare workers who dealt with your client on 1 and 10 April 2000 were very concerned about her children's welfare because of your client's drunkenness and obvious psychiatric instability. Even without the issue of the syphilis, a reference to the Child Protection Unit would have been made. No court would be likely to conclude that the disclosure about syphilis would be conclusive of the children's fate one way or another. If she loses the children, she would have lost them anyway. In that case the issue of the syphilis is causally irrelevant. If she keeps the children, the issue of the syphilis is causally irrelevant.

We note your comments about the *Data Protection Act 1998* and do not place the same construction on its provisions. You will have to try your luck in court with that claim.

Your request for an undertaking that there be no further disclosure is unnecessary. We can confirm that it is not intended that there be any further disclosure.

The Trust has done everything necessary to discharge what it (legally correctly) sees as its public duty of disclosure.

If you manage to obtain an interim injunction, we will attend by counsel on the return date and are confident that it will be discharged with costs against your client. If you pursue an action for damages/a permanent injunction, it will be vigorously resisted.

We confirm that we are instructed to accept service on behalf of the Trust.

8.3   **Claimant's letter in response**

Cry, Woolf & Co,
High St,
Thatsit,
Deathshire

Messrs Offhook,
Swishpad Lane,
Hugefees,
London SW1

14 April 2000

Re Your client Mrs Viola Ted, dob 3.4.1967
Our client, the Deathshire NHS Trust

Thank you for your faxed letter of today's date.

Jeffreys J, sitting in chambers in the Queen's Bench Division, was not as unimpressed by our client's case as you were. Enclosed herewith, by way of service, is the order he made restraining your client from any further relevant disclosure.

A return date of 21 April 2000 at 10.30am has been fixed at which you will be able to put your side of the story.

We have to point out that your side of the story (if factually true, which we wholly dispute), does not have the legal effect you contend for.

First, the mere mention in the hearing of the other people in the waiting room of the issue of the syphilis does not mean that that information has lost its confidential character. The test which the court is likely to apply (although we accept that this has not yet been definitively decided in this jurisdiction), is whether our client would reasonably have expected the people in the waiting room to pass on the information to others in such a way as to produce the mischief (communication to the social services and so on) which actually occurred in this case. Of course we accept that if information has become genuinely public knowledge (for instance by publication in a high circulation newspaper or by a broadcast on television) it loses its confidential nature. But that is a million miles from an incoherently drunken mention to a few gynaecological patients in a small District Hospital.

Exactly the same comment applies to what you grandly refer to as our client's disclaimer of any rights she might otherwise have in confidential information. Had she sold her story to the newspaper, that would be true. But she has not. There is no even remotely arguable parallel between the two situations.

We expected you to take the *Egdell* point. We are not concerned by it. The courts are notoriously protective of confidences in a medical context. Of course the public interest in disclosure has to be balanced against the public interest in maintaining confidentiality. The public interest in encouraging patients to be frank with their doctors hugely outweighs the arguable public interest of disclosure of the information which was disclosed here. This is an *X v Y* case, (see [1988] 2 All ER 648) not an *Egdell* case.

Your points on causation are curious. The courts are ready to infer detriment from the mere fact of unlawful disclosure. We refer you to *A-G v Guardian Newspapers Ltd (No 2)* [1990] AC 109, per Lord Keith at p256.

8.4   **Particulars of claim in a breach of confidentiality case**
In the High Court of Justice   Claim No
Queen's Bench Division

Between:

Viola Ted   Claimant
and
(1) Ian Discreet
(2) Deathshire Hospital NHS Trust
(3) Ms Beastly Kidgrab
(4) Deathshire Social Services Defendants

Particulars of Claim

---

1. At all material times:
    1. The First Defendant was a Consultant Obste-
        trician & Gynaecologist, employed or engaged
        by the Second Defendant;
    2. The Third Defendant was employed by the
        Fourth Defendant in its Child Protection Unit.
2. On or about 1 April 2000 the Claimant attended
    the Outpatient Clinic at the premises of the
    Second Defendant and consulted the First Defen-
    dant in the course of his engagement.
3. During the course of the consultation the Claim-
    ant indicated her concern that she may have con-
    tracted syphilis in the course of an extra-marital
    affair. The First Defendant took swabs and blood
    samples, which were reported on 4 April 2000.
    The diagnosis was communicated to the Claimant
    by the First Defendant at an Outpatient appoint-
    ment on 10 April 2000.
4. By letter dated 13 April 2000 the First Defendant
    wrote to the Fourth Defendant advising the
    Fourth Defendant, its servants and/or agents to:
    1. Tell the Claimant to inform her husband about
        her diagnosis so that he could be screened and,
        if necessary, treated for syphilis;

2. In the event that the Claimant failed to inform her husband, to take steps to inform him directly and;

3. Arrange for the Claimant's children to be taken into care, because the circumstances in which the infection was acquired indicated that she was not fit to be a mother.

5. On the morning of 14 April the Third Defendant attended at the Claimant's address and communicated the terms of the above letter to the Claimant.

6. The information set out in Paragraph 3 above was communicated to the First Defendant in circumstances of confidence and was disseminated by him in breach of confidence.

7. Further or alternatively, the First Defendant disseminated the said information in breach of the Claimant's right to respect for her private and family life and home pursuant to Article 8(1) of the European Convention on Human Rights.

8. Further or alternatively, the First Defendant, by disclosing the said information, processed sensitive personal data in respect of the Claimant in breach of the data protection principles pursuant to the Data Protection Act 1998.

9. By reason of the First Defendant's breach of confidence, the Claimant has suffered distress, loss and damage.

10. Further or alternatively, the Claimant fears that, unless restrained, the Defendants and each of them will further disseminate the said information in breach of confidence.

11. Further the Claimant is entitled to interest pursuant to s69 of the County Courts Act 1984; further or alternatively pursuant to the equitable jurisdiction of the Court at such rate and for such period as the Court shall deem just.

12. The likely value of this action exceeds £15,000.

AND the Claimant claims:
1. Damages for breach of confidence;
2. A permanent injunction restraining the Defendants and each of them whether by themselves, their servants and/or agents from communicating, passing on or otherwise disseminating in any way to any person any information which: (i) concerns the Claimant's medical condition; (ii) relates to her suitability to be a mother; (iii) was communicated by the Claimant in circumstances of confidentiality;
3. Interest pursuant to s69 of the County Courts Act 1984 further or alternatively pursuant to the equitable jurisdiction of the Court.

[Statement of Truth]

Dated etc

8.5   **Interim injunction order in a breach of confidentiality case**

In the High Court of Justice   Claim No
Queen's Bench Division
Mr Justice Jeffreys
Between:

Viola Ted	Claimant
and	
(1) Ian Discreet	
(2) Deathshire Hospital NHS Trust	
(3) Ms Beastly Kidgrab	
(4) Deathshire Social Services	Defendants

_____

Order

_____

Upon Hearing Counsel for the Claimant without notice and upon considering the Particulars of Claim annexed hereto;

It Is Ordered That:

1. The Defendants and each of them are hereby restrained until further Order whether by themselves, their servants and/or agents or otherwise from communicating, passing on or otherwise disseminating in any way to any person any information which: (i) concerns the Claimant's medical condition; (ii) relates to her suitability to be a mother; (iii) was communicated by the Claimant in circumstances of confidentiality;
2. This matter be listed before the Judge in Private on notice on 23 April 2000 at 10.30am.

Dated this 16 day of April 2000

8.6   **Defence in a breach of confidentiality case**
In the High Court of Justice   Claim No
Queen's Bench Division
Between:

Viola Ted   Claimant
and
(1) Ian Discreet
(2) Deathshire Hospital NHS Trust
(3) Ms Beastly Kidgrab
(4) Deathshire Social Services Defendants

Defence of the First and Second Defendants

1. Paragraph 1(1) of the Particulars of Claim is admitted. Save as aforesaid the First and Second Defendants do not plead to Paragraph 1.
2. It is admitted and/or averred that:
    (a) On 1 April 2000 the Claimant attended the Outpatient Department of the Deathshire Hospital, waiting for an appointment with the First Defendant;
    (b) The Claimant was drunk;

(c) Whilst in the waiting room the Claimant shouted loudly to the crowd of patients words to the effect of: 'I've got syphilis and I don't care who knows it. I got it from Ian Pus, and it was worth every penny.';

(d) During the consultation with the First Defendant, the Claimant repeated the above. She also told the First Defendant that the disliked her husband and that, although she had not yet had sexual intercourse with her husband since her affair with Ian Pus, she intended to resume normal sexual relations with her husband imminently with the express intention of infecting him with syphilis;

(e) Further, during the consultation, the First Defendant noted a number of suppurating syphilitic sores on the Claimant's hands. He was extremely concerned about the possibility that the Claimant's children might be infected too;

(f) Accordingly the First Defendant wrote to the Fourth Defendant in the terms pleaded.

Save as aforesaid, no admissions are made as to Paragraphs 2 to 4 inclusive.

3.   No admissions are made as to Paragraph 5.

4.   Paragraph 6 is denied. The information was not, alternatively was no longer, confidential information and the Claimant disclaimed any rights she might otherwise have had in relation to further disclosure.

5.   Further or alternatively, any disclosure by the First Defendant was in the course of his engagement as a doctor and was in the public interest.

6.   Paragraph 7 is denied. The First Defendant's disclosure of the said information was in accordance with the law and necessary in a democratic society in the interests of public safety, for the prevention of crime, for the protection of health and morals and for the protection of the rights and freedoms of others pursuant to Article 8(2).

7. No admissions are made as to Paragraphs 8 and/or 9.

8. Paragraph 10 is denied. The First and Second Defendant, having discharged their legal duties as aforesaid, have no intention of making any further disclosure.

9. No admissions are made as to Paragraphs 11 and/or 12.

[Statement of Truth]

Dated etc

Appendix 1:
The General Medical Council's Guidelines on Confidentiality

Guidelines about confidentiality come in three of the GMC's publications. These are:

(a) *Good Medical Practice*, which 'sets out the basic principles of good practice.' The booklet emphasises that it provides '... guidance. It is not a set of rules, nor is it exhaustive. The GMC publishes more detailed guidance on confidentiality ... and the ethical problems surrounding HIV and AIDS.'

(b) *Confidentiality*, which 'sets out the GMC's guidance on confidentiality. It enlarges on the principles described in the booklet *Good Medical Practice*.'

(c) *Serious Communicable Diseases* which 'expands on [the advice given in *Good Medical Practice*] in relation to the treatment of patients with serious communicable diseases and the responsibilities of doctors who have or may have such diseases.'

All these publications are available from the GMC at the address given in Appendix 8.

Good Medical Practice

Clause 16: Confidentiality

'Patients have a right to expect that you will not pass on any personal information which you learn in the course of your professional duties, unless they agree. If in exceptional circumstances you feel you should pass on information without a patient's consent, or against a patient's wishes, you should read our booklet *Confidentiality* and be prepared to justify your decision.'

Confidentiality

'Principles of confidentiality

1. Patients have a right to expect that you will not disclose any personal information which you learn during the course of your professional duties, unless they give permission. Without assurances about confidentiality patients may be reluctant to give doctors the information they need in order to provide good care. For these reasons:

    - When you are responsible for confidential information you must make sure that the information is effectively protected against improper disclosure when it is disposed of, stored, transmitted or received;

    - When patients give consent to disclosure of information about them, you must make sure they understand what will be disclosed, the reasons for the disclosure and the likely consequences.

    - You must make sure that patients are informed whenever information about them is likely to be disclosed to others involved in their health care, and that they have the opportunity to withhold permission;

    - You must respect requests by patients that information should not be disclosed to third parties, save in exceptional circumstances (for example where the health or safety of others would otherwise be at serious risk);

    - If you disclose confidential information you should release only as much information as is necessary for the purpose;

    - You must make sure that health workers to whom you disclose information understand that it is given to them in confidence which they must respect;

– If you decide to disclose confidential information, you must be prepared to explain and justify your decision.

These principles apply in all circumstances, including those discussed in this booklet.

Disclosure of confidential information with the patient's consent

2.   You may release confidential information in strict accordance with the patient's consent, or the consent of a person properly authorised to act on the patient's behalf.

Disclosure within teams

3.   Modern medical practice usually involves teams of doctors, other healthcare workers, and sometimes people from outside the healthcare professions. The importance of working in teams is explained in the GMC's booklet *Good Medical Practice*. To provide patients with the best possible care, it is often essential to pass confidential information between members of the team.

4.   You should make sure – through the use of leaflets and posters if necessary – that patients understand why and when information may be shared between team members, and any circumstances in which team members providing non-medical care may be required to disclose information to third parties.

5.   Where the disclosure of relevant information between healthcare professionals is clearly required for treatment to which a patient has agreed, the patient's explicit consent may not be required. For example, explicit consent would not be needed where a general practitioner discloses relevant information to a medical secretary to have a referral letter typed, or a physician makes relevant information available to a radiologist when requesting an x-ray.

6.   There will also be circumstances where, because of a medical emergency, a patient's consent cannot be obtained, but relevant information must in the

patient's interest be transferred between healthcare workers.

7. If a patient does not wish you to share particular information with other members of the team, you must respect those wishes. If you and a patient have established a relationship based on trust, the patient may choose to give you discretion to disclose information to other team members, as required.

8. All medical members of a team have a duty to make sure that other team members understand and observe confidentiality.

Disclosure to employers and insurance companies

9. When assessing a patient on behalf of a third party (for example, an employer or insurance company) you must make sure, at the outset, that the patient is aware of the purpose of the assessment, of the obligation that the doctor has towards the third parties concerned, and that this may necessitate the disclosure of personal information. You should undertake such assessment only with the patient's written consent.

Disclosure of information without the patient's consent

Disclosure in the patient's medical interests

10. Problems may arise if you consider that a patient is incapable of giving consent to treatment because of immaturity, illness, or mental incapacity, and you have tried unsuccessfully to persuade the patient to allow an appropriate person to be involved in the consultation. If you are convinced that it is essential in the patient's medical interests, you may disclose relevant information to an appropriate person or authority. You must tell the patient before disclosing any information. You should remember that the judgment of whether patients are capable of giving or withholding consent to treatment or disclosure must be based on an assessment of their ability to appreciate what the treatment or advice being sought may involve, and not solely on their age.

11.   If you believe a patient to be a victim of neglect or physical or sexual abuse, and unable to give or withhold consent to disclosure, you should usually give information to an appropriate responsible person or statutory agency, in order to prevent further harm to the patient. In these and similar circumstances, you may release information without the patient's consent, but only if you consider that the patient is unable to give consent, and that the disclosure is in the patient's best medical interests.

12.   Rarely, you may judge that seeking consent to the disclosure of confidential information would be damaging to the patient, but that the disclosure would be in the patient's medical interests. For example, you may judge that it would be in a patient's interests that a close relative should know about the patient's terminal condition, but that the patient would be seriously harmed by the information. In such circumstances information may be disclosed without consent.

Disclosure after a patient's death

13.   You still have an obligation to keep information confidential after a patient dies. The extent to which confidential information may be disclosed after a patient's death will depend on the circumstances. These include the nature of the information, whether that information is already public knowledge, and how long it is since the patient died. Particular difficulties may arise when there is a conflict of interest between parties affected by the patient's death. For example, if an insurance company seeks information about a deceased patient in order to decide whether to make a payment under a life assurance policy, you should not release information without the consent of the patient's executor, or a close relative, who has been fully informed of the consequences of disclosure.

14.   You should be aware that the Access to Health Records Act 1990 gives third parties right of access, in certain

circumstances, to the medical records of a deceased patient.

Disclosure for medical teaching, medical research, and medical audit

Research

15.	Where, for the purposes of medical research there is a need to disclose information which it is not possible to anonymise effectively, every reasonable effort must be made to inform the patients concerned, or those who may properly give permission on their behalf, that they may, at any stage, withhold their consent to disclosure.

16.	Where consent cannot be obtained, this fact should be drawn to the attention of a research ethics committee which should decide whether the public interest in the research outweighs patients' rights to confidentiality. Disclosures to a researcher may otherwise be improper, even if the researcher is a registered medical practitioner.

Teaching and audit

17.	Patients' consent to disclosure of information for teaching and audit must be obtained unless the data have been effectively anonymised.

Disclosure in the interests of others

18.	Disclosures may be necessary in the public interest where a failure to disclose information may expose the patient, or others, to risk of death or serious harm. In such circumstances you should disclose information promptly to an appropriate person or authority.

19.	Such circumstances may arise, for example, where:
	– a patient continues to drive, against medical advice, when unfit to do so. In such circumstances you should disclose relevant information to the medical adviser of the Driver and Vehicle Licensing Agency without delay. Further guidance is given in appendix 1.
	– a colleague, who is also a patient, is placing patients at risk as a result of illness or another medical condition. Guidance on this issue, and on the rights of

doctors who are ill, is contained in the GMC's leaflet *Serious Communicable Diseases* and in a separate note about the GMC's health procedures.

– disclosure is necessary for the prevention or detection of a serious crime.

Disclosure in connection with judicial or other statutory proceedings

20. You may disclose information to satisfy a specific statutory requirement, such as notification of a communicable disease or of attendance upon a person dependent upon certain controlled drugs. You may also disclose information if ordered to do so by a judge or presiding officer of a court, or if you are summoned to assist a Coroner, Procurator Fiscal, or other similar officer in connection with an inquest or comparable judicial investigation. If you are required to produce patients' notes or records under a court order you should disclose only so much as is relevant to the proceedings. You should object to the judge or the presiding officer if attempts are made to compel you to disclose other matters which appear in the notes, for example matters relating to relatives or partners of the patient who are not parties to the proceedings.

21. In the absence of a court order, a request for disclosure by a third party, for example, a solicitor, police officer, or officer of a court, is not sufficient justification for disclosure without a patient's consent.

22. When a Committee of the GMC investigating a doctor's fitness to practice has determined that the interests of justice require disclosure of confidential information, you may disclose information at the request of the Committee's Chairman, provided that every reasonable effort has been made to seek the consent of the patients concerned. If consent is refused the patient's wishes must be respected.

Disclosure to inspectors of taxes

23. If you have a private practice, you may disclose confidential information in response to a request from an inspector of taxes, provided you have made every

effort to separate financial information from clinical records.

Doctors who decide to disclose confidential information must be prepared to explain and justify their decisions.

Appendix 1

Disclosure of information about patients to the Driver and Vehicle Licensing Agency (DVLA)

1. The DVLA is legally responsible for deciding if a person is medically unfit to drive. They need to know when driving licence holders have a condition which may now, or in the future, affect their safety as a driver.

2. Therefore, when patients have such conditions you should:
    - make sure that the patients understand that the condition may impair their ability to drive. If a driver is incapable of understanding this advice, for example because of dementia, you should inform the DVLA immediately.
    - explain to patients that they have a legal duty to inform the DVLA about the condition.

3. If the patients refuse to accept the diagnosis or the effect of the condition on their ability to drive, you can suggest that the patients seek a second opinion, and make appropriate arrangements for the patients to do so. You should advise patients not to drive until the second opinion has been obtained.

4. If patients continue to drive when they are not fit to do so, you should make every reasonable effort to persuade them to stop. This may include telling their next of kin.

5. If you do not manage to persuade patients to stop driving, or you are given or find evidence that a patient is continuing to drive contrary to advice, you should disclose relevant medical information immediately, in confidence, to the medical adviser at the DVLA.

6.   Before giving information to the DVLA you should
            inform the patient of your decision to do so. Once the
            DVLA has been informed, you should also write to the
            patient, to confirm that a disclosure has been made.'

Serious Communicable Diseases

'... In this guidance the term serious communicable
disease applies to any disease which may be transmitted
from human to human and which may result in death
or serious illness. It particularly concerns, but is not
limited to, infections such as human immunodeficiency
virus (HIV), tuberculosis and hepatitis B and C ...

Confidentiality

Informing other health care professionals

18.   If you diagnose a patient as having a serious communi-
            cable disease, you should explain to the patient:
            – the nature of the disease and its medical, social and
              occupational implications, as appropriate.
            – ways of protecting others from infection.
            – the importance of giving the professionals who will
              be providing care information which they need to
              know about the patient's disease or condition. In
              particular you must make sure the patient under-
              stands that general practitioners cannot provide ade-
              quate clinical management without knowledge of
              their patients' conditions.

19.   If patients still refuse to allow other healthcare workers
            to be informed, you must respect the patients' wishes
            except where you judge that failure to disclose the
            information would put a healthcare worker or other
            patient at serious risk of death or serious harm. Such
            situations may arise, for example, when dealing with
            violent patients with severe mental illness or disability.
            If you are in doubt about whether disclosure is appro-
            priate, you should seek advice from an experienced
            colleague. You should inform patients before disclos-
            ing information. Such occasions are likely to arise

rarely and you must be prepared to justify a decision to disclose information against a patient's wishes.

Disclosures to others

20.   You must disclose information about serious communicable diseases in accordance with the law. For example, the appropriate authority must be informed where a notifiable disease is diagnosed. Where a communicable disease has contributed to the cause of death, this must be recorded on the death certificate. You should also pass information about serious communicable diseases to the relevant authorities for the purpose of communicable disease control and surveillance.

21.   As the GMC booklet *Confidentiality* makes clear, a patient's death does not, of itself, release a doctor from the obligation to maintain confidentiality. But in some circumstances disclosures can be justified because they protect other people from serious harm or because they are required by law.

Giving information to close contacts

22.   You may disclose information about a patient, whether living or dead, in order to protect a patient from risk of death or serious harm. For example, you may disclose information to a known sexual contact of a patient with HIV where you have reason to think that the patient has not informed that person, and cannot be persuaded to do so. In such circumstances you should tell the patient before you make the disclosure, and you must be prepared to justify a decision to disclose information.

23.   You must not disclose information to others, for example relatives, who have not been, and are not, at risk of infection ...

Treating colleagues with serious communicable diseases

34.   If you are treating a doctor or other health worker with a serious communicable disease you must provide the

confidentiality and support to which every patient is entitled.

35.   If you know, or have good reason to believe, that a medical colleague or healthcare worker who has, or may have, a serious communicable disease, is practising, or has practised, in a way which places patients at risk, you must inform an appropriate person in the healthcare worker's employing authority, for example an occupational healthcare physician, or, where appropriate, the relevant regulatory body. Such cases are likely to arise very rarely. Wherever possible you should inform the healthcare worker concerned before passing information to an employer or regulatory body.'

These extracts have been reproduced with the kind permission of the General Medical Council.

Appendix 2:
The General Dental Council's Guidelines on Confidentiality

These are contained in the GDC's publication *Maintaining Standards: Guidelines to Dentists on Professional and Personal Conduct*.

Maintaining confidentiality

'The dentist/patient relationship is founded on trust and a dentist should not disclose to a third party information about a patient acquired in a professional capacity without the permission of the patient. To do so may lead to a charge of serious professional misconduct. A dentist should also be aware that the duty of confidentiality extends to other members of the dental team.

Where information is held on computer, a dentist should also have regard to the provisions of the Data Protection Act.

There may, however, be circumstances in which the public interest outweighs a dentist's duty of confidentiality and in which disclosure would be justified. A dentist in such a situation should consult a defence organisation or other professional adviser.

Communications with patients should not compromise patient confidentiality. In the interests of security and confidentiality, for example, it is advisable that all postal communications to patients are sent in sealed envelopes.'

Dental records and radiographs

> 'Patient records, including radiographs and study models, provide valuable information as to the treatment carried out and, where possible, should be retained.
>
> A dentist with computerized patient records must ensure that the computer system used includes appropriate features to safeguard the security and integrity of those records.
>
> The Data Protection Act 1984, which covers computer-held records made at any time, gives the patient the right to see and/or have copies of computer-held records. The Access to Health Records Act 1990 gives the same rights to patients concerning manual records made after 1 November 1991.'

Disposal of patient records

> 'In view of the confidentiality of patient records, at the time of disposal they must be disposed of securely, usually by incineration or shredding.'

The GDC's guidance is subject to revision from time to time. The GDC should be contacted for the most recent text before reliance is placed on these extracts.

These extracts are reproduced with the kind permission of the General Dental Council.

Appendix 3:
The United Kingdom Central Council for Nursing, Midwifery and Health Visiting (UKCC) Guidelines on Confidentiality

The UKCC produces guidelines which apply to nurses, midwives and health visitors. There is a Code of Professional Conduct, but the most useful guidelines appear in its publication: *Guidelines for Professional Practice*.

Confidentiality

'To trust another person with private and personal information about yourself is a significant matter. If the person to whom that information is given is a nurse, midwife or health visitor, the patient or client has the right to believe that this information, given in confidence, will only be used for the purposes for which it was given and will not be released to others without their permission. The death of a patient or client does not give you the right to break confidentiality.'

Clause 10 of the Code of Professional Conduct addresses the subject directly. It states that:

'As a registered nurse, midwife or health visitor, you are personally accountable for your practice and, in the exercise of your professional accountability, must ...

10. Protect all confidential information concerning patients and clients obtained in the course of

professional practice and make disclosures only with consent, where required by the order of a court or where you can justify disclosure in the wider public interest.

Confidentiality should only be broken in exceptional circumstances and should only occur after careful consideration that you can justify your actions.

It is impractical to obtain the consent of the patient or client every time you need to share information with other health professionals or other staff involved in the healthcare of that patient or client. What is important is that the patient or client understands that some information may be made available to others involved in the delivery of their care. However, the patient or client must know who the information will be shared with.

Patients and clients have a right to know the standards of confidentiality maintained by those providing their care, and these standards should be made known by the health professional at the first point of contact. These standards of confidentiality can be reinforced by leaflets and posters where the healthcare is being delivered.

Providing information

You always need to obtain the explicit consent of a patient or client before you disclose specific information and you must make sure that the patient or client can make an informed response as to whether that information can be disclosed.

Disclosure of information occurs:
* with the consent of the patient or client;
* without the consent of the patient or client when the disclosure is required by law or by order of a court; and
* without the consent of the patient or client when the disclosure is considered to be necessary in the public interest.

The *public interest* means the interests of an individual, or groups of individuals, or of society as a whole, and would, for example, cover matters such as serious crime, child abuse, drug trafficking or other activities which place others at serious risk.

There is no statutory right to confidentiality, but an aggrieved individual can sue through a civil court alleging that confidentiality was broken.

The situation that causes most problems is when your decision to withhold confidential information or give it to a third party has serious consequences. The information may have been given to you in the strictest confidence by a patient, or a client, or by a colleague. You could also discover the information in the course of your work.

You may sometimes be under pressure to release information but you must realise that you will be held accountable for this. In all cases where you deliberately release information in what you believe to be the best interests of the public, your decision must be justified. In some circumstances, such as accident and emergency admissions where the police are involved, it may be appropriate to involve senior staff if you do not feel that you are able to deal with the situation alone.

The above circumstances can be particularly stressful, especially if vulnerable groups are concerned, as releasing information may mean that a third party becomes involved, as in the case of children or those with learning difficulties.

You should always discuss the matter fully with other professional colleagues and, if appropriate, consult the UKCC or a membership organisation before making the decision to release information without a patient's permission. There will often be significant consequences which you must consider carefully before you make the decision to withhold or release information. Having made a decision, you should write down the reason either in the appropriate record or in a special note that can be kept in a separate file (outlined in the UKCC's booklet *Standards for Records and Record-keeping*). You then have written justification for the action which you took if this becomes necessary and you can also review the decision later in the light of future developments.

Ownership of and access to records

Organisations which employ professional staff who make records are the legal owners of these records but that does not give anyone in that organisation the legal right of access to the information in those records. However, the patient or client can ask to see their records, whether they are written down or on computer. This is as a result of the Data Protection Act 1984 (Access Modification) (Health) Order 1987 and the Access to Health Records Act 1990.

The Contracts of Employment of all employees not directly involved with patients but who have access to or handle confidential records should contain clauses which emphasise the principles of confidentiality and state the disciplinary action which could result if these principles are not met.

As far as computer-held records are concerned, you must be satisfied that as far as possible, the methods you use for recording information are secure. You must also find out which categories of staff have access to records to which they are expected to contribute important personal and confidential information. Local procedures must include ways to check whether a record is authentic when there is no written signature. All records must wholly indicate the identity of the person who made that record. As more patient and client records are moved and linked between healthcare settings by computer, you have to be vigilant in order to make sure that patient or client confidentiality is not broken. This means trying to ensure that the systems used are protected from inappropriate access within your direct area of practice, for example, ensuring that personal access codes are kept secure.

The Computer Misuse Act 1990 came into force to secure computer programmes and data against unauthorised access to alteration. Authorised users have permission to use certain programmes and data.

If those users go beyond what is permitted, this is a criminal offence. The Act makes provision for accidentally exceeding your permission and covers fraud, extortion and blackmail.

Where access to information contained on a computer filing system is available to members of staff who are not registered practitioners, or health professionals governed by similar ethical principles, an important clause concerning confidentiality should appear within their Contract of Employment (outlined in the UKCC's position statement: *Confidentiality: Use of Computers 1994*).

Those who receive confidential information from a patient or client should advise them that the information will be given to the registered practitioner involved in their care. If necessary, this may also include other professionals in the health and social work fields. Registered practitioners must make sure that, where possible, the storage and movement of records within the healthcare setting does not put the confidentiality of patient information at risk.

Access to records for teaching, research and audit

If patients' or clients' records need to be used to help students gain the knowledge and skills which they require, the same principles of confidentiality apply to the information. This also applies to those engaged in research and audit. The manager of the healthcare setting is responsible for the security of the information contained in these records and for making sure that access to the information is closely supervised. The person providing the training will be responsible for making sure that the students understand the need for confidentiality and the need to follow local procedures for handling and storing records. The patient or client should know about the individual having access to their records and should be able to refuse that access if they wish.

These extracts are reproduced with the kind permission of the UK Central Council for Nursing, Midwifery and Health Visiting.

Appendix 4:
The Chartered Society of Physiotherapy's Guidelines on Confidentiality

These are contained in the Society's publication *Rules of Professional Conduct.*

Confidentiality

'Chartered physiotherapists shall ensure the confidentiality and security of information acquired in a professional capacity.

This rule is intended to guide members on their responsibilities in relation to the confidentiality and security of information gained by them in the course of their practice. Basically all information gained by a therapist about a patient is confidential: this includes the fact that a patient is attending for treatment. So the confirmation of an appointment and/or notification of attendance is also confidential. (For example if a telephone call is received in a physiotherapy department making enquiries about the attendance record of a particular patient, unless the physiotherapist is confident that they recognise the voice of an anxious relative, the caller must be informed that no information about the patient can be divulged. To do so could result in a claim of breaching this rule.)

It is also important that any non-qualified personnel involved with patients, such as assistants, receptionists and clerical staff in physiotherapy departments and private practices, are aware that information passed to them by patients is confidential.

Such information is not to be divulged to a third party without the consent (preferably in writing) of the patient unless the Chartered Physiotherapist is required to do so under statutory authority or so directed by a competent legal authority such as a judge, or where it is necessary to protect the welfare of the patient or to prevent harm, or it is (rarely) justified in the public interest. If there is doubt the Chartered Physiotherapist should seek advice.

However, there are occasions when important information may be given to the Chartered Physiotherapist by a patient because of the relationship which exists between them. In such cases, the position must be explained to the patient and their permission requested to pass on what is relevant or vital, either to another member of the healthcare team or to an appropriate authority.

This rule also applies to any information that is obtained during audit, a research project, or clinical examination or peer review procedure, which may identify individual patients, unless written consent is obtained. Use of photographs, videos or other visual material must always have written consent and wherever possible such material should be anonymised (but merely blanking out the eyes of a facial photograph is not acceptable).

It may also come to the attention of the physiotherapist that a patient is proposing to undertake an activity which because of their clinical and/or other condition could be harmful to themselves and/or others such as driving or operating potentially dangerous machinery. The physiotherapist must try and persuade the patient not to undertake this activity. If necessary they will make a report to the patient's doctor or other relevant authority having first informed the patient.

Information not related to the patient's social or medical condition

Some of this information may be very personal, but whether it is or not, all this information is confidential, that is, it cannot and must not be discussed with others. Most of it need not be recorded but may give insight into the patient's view of and response to physiotherapy, and may affect the approach adopted by the physiotherapist. Some information which is not clinically significant on initial assessment may assume a greater significance at a later date.

Other people may have information about the patient or their family which members may consider necessary for them to know.

Should at any time Chartered Physiotherapists breach confidentiality for whatever reasons, they must be prepared to justify their actions under this rule.

The multi-professional team

Much valuable and necessary information is exchanged within multi-professional team meetings. However, it is still not usual for the patient/client to be present during such a conference and she/he is often unaware that such a conference is being held. It is therefore important that all members of the team are aware that confidential information is being exchanged. Only relevant and factual information can be divulged, and no 'gossip' can take place. It may also be appropriate that meetings are arranged in such a way that *only* the professionals involved with the care of that patient are involved in the discussion. If a patient and/or their carers have not been involved in the conference a named person should be identified to report back to the patient.

Requests for Information

From the patient

In some cases, patients are unaware of their diagnosis, eg carcinoma or chronic degenerating neurophysiological condition such as multiple sclerosis or Parkinson's disease. Patients may be unsure as to why they have been referred for physiotherapy and ask the physiotherapists for their diagnosis. Members are reminded that such information should only be given to the patient by the doctor with overall responsibility for the patient. Members are therefore advised not to give such information but to contact that doctor and inform him/her that the patient is requesting it; also, if necessary, indicating the dilemma faced by the physio-therapists with a patient who does not know the reason for referral to physiotherapy. This also applies to the results of tests outside those relating to physio-therapy.

From neighbours and other patients

With patients both in hospital and in the community, the physiotherapist is often the common factor, and may receive enquiries about other patients and neigh-bours. Physio-therapists must be vigilant to ensure that they do not disclose any confidential information.

From official sources such as DSS, solicitors, etc

Before disclosing any information, check that the patient has given written permission for such informa-tion to be disclosed. The Society's *Legal Work Pack* pro-vides further advice regarding disclosing information to members of the legal profession.

From supervisors/managers' employers

Before disclosing any information, check that the patient understands what information will be given and the need for the disclosure of such information. Employers may contact the physiotherapy department to check on attendance; this information is confidential and may not be disclosed.

Other competent authorities

The nature of the authority should be verified and the patient's permission sought prior to disclosing infor-mation.

Extraneous information

The following are some examples of informa-tion/knowledge that physiotherapists acquire in the course of their practice, and some ideas on how to deal with them.

- *Knowledge of criminal activities:* a physiotherapist recently became aware, when visiting a patient, of discussions going on in an adjoining room regarding robbing a local bank. After discussion with the line manager the police were informed.

- *Evidence of abuse:* physical, sexual or psychological – not necessarily of the patient being treated. This is often very difficult to deal with but urgent discussions with a senior colleague with the relevant referral to an appropriate professional such as a doctor, or a health visitor, or agency such as Social Services are essential. The Children Act gives clear guidance to professionals when abuse of children is discovered.

- *Environmental issues:* where there is evidence of environmental problems such as infestation by fleas or mice, or excessive damp or structural damage, members should inform their service manager, the relevant doctor, or other appropriate authority.'

These extracts are reproduced with the kind permission of the Chartered Society of Pysiotherapy.

Appendix 5:
The Royal College of Veterinary Surgeons' Guidelines on Confidentiality

These are set out in the Royal College of Veterinary Surgeons *Guide to Professional Conduct 2000*.

One of the 'ten guiding principles' of the *Code of Professional Practice* is that:

'Your clients are entitled to expect that you will ... foster and maintain a good relationship with your clients, earning their trust, respecting their views and protecting client confidentiality ...'

The Code later emphasises that:

'The professional/client relationship is one of mutual trust and respect under which a veterinary surgeon must: maintain client confidentiality ...'

Under the heading *Disclosure of Information* there appears the following:

Client confidentiality

'The veterinary surgeon's/client relationship is founded on trust, and in normal circumstances a veterinary surgeon must not disclose to any third party any information about a client of their animal either given by the client, or revealed by clinical examination or by postmortem examination. This duty also extends to associated support staff.

In circumstances where the client has not given permission for disclosure and when the veterinary surgeon believes that animal welfare or public interest are compromised, the RCVS should be consulted before any information is divulged.

Permission to pass on confidential information may be express or implied. Express permission may be either verbal or in writing, usually in response to a request. Permission may also be implied from circumstances, for example in the making of a claim under a pet insurance policy, when the insurance company becomes entitled to receive all information relevant to the claim and to seek clarification if required.

Registration of a dog with the Kennel Club permits a veterinary surgeon who carries out surgery to alter the natural confirmation of a dog, to report this to the Kennel Club.'

Case Records

Case records, including radiograph films and similar documents, are the property of, and should be retained by, veterinary surgeons in the interests of animal welfare and for their own protection. Copies with a summary of the history should be passed on request to a colleague taking over the case. (NB: Where a client has been specifically charged and has paid for radiographs or other reports, they are legally entitled to them. The practice may, however, choose to make it clear that they are charging not for the radiographs, but for a diagnosis or advice only. In appropriate circumstances they may be prepared also to provide copies of the radiographs.)'

The Data Protection Acts 1984 and 1999 (sic) give anyone the right to be informed about any personal data relating to themselves on payment of an administration charge.

It should also be recognised that clients who now have access to their own medical records are likely to seek similar access to their pets records. In such cases it may be helpful for a client to be offered sight of the records at the surgery, by appointment, at a mutually convenient time.

It follows that the utmost care is essential in writing case notes or recording a client's personal details to ensure that the latter are accurate (particularly in relation to financial details) and that the notes are comprehensible and legible.

Disclosure of records may be ordered in disciplinary or court hearings, and the RCVS may require copies of case records routinely in the course of investigating a complaint.'

These extracts are reproduced with the kind permission of the Royal College of Veterinary Surgeons.

Appendix 6:
The Data Protection Act 1998 (Extracts)

Part I Preliminary

Basic interpretative provisions.

1. – (1)   In this Act, unless the context otherwise requires –
'data' means information which –

(a)   is being processed by means of equipment operating automatically in response to instructions given for that purpose,

(b)   is recorded with the intention that it should be processed by means of such equipment,

(c)   is recorded as part of a relevant filing system or with the intention that it should form part of a relevant filing system, or

(d)   does not fall within paragraph (a), (b) or (c) but forms part of an accessible record as defined by s68;

'data controller' means, subject to subsection (4), a person who (either alone or jointly or in common with other persons) determines the purposes for which and the manner in which any personal data are, or are to be, processed;

'data processor', in relation to personal data, means any person (other than an employee of the data controller) who processes the data on behalf of the data controller;

'data subject' means an individual who is the subject of personal data;

'personal data' means data which relate to a living individual who can be identified –

(a)   from those data, or

(b)   from those data and other information which is in the possession of, or is likely to come into the possession of, the data controller,

and includes any expression of opinion about the individual and any indication of the intentions of the data controller or any other person in respect of the individual;

'processing', in relation to information or data, means obtaining, recording or holding the information or data or carrying out any operation or set of operations on the information or data, including –

(a)   organisation, adaptation or alteration of the information or data,

(b)   retrieval, consultation or use of the information or data,

(c)   disclosure of the information or data by transmission, dissemination or otherwise making available, or

(d)   alignment, combination, blocking, erasure or destruction of the information or data;

'relevant filing system' means any set of information relating to individuals to the extent that, although the information is not processed by means of equipment operating automatically in response to instructions given for that purpose, the set is structured, either by reference to individuals or by reference to criteria relating to individuals, in such a way that specific information relating to a particular individual is readily accessible.

(2)   In this Act, unless the context otherwise requires –

(a)   'obtaining' or 'recording', in relation to personal data, includes obtaining or recording the information to be contained in the data, and

(b) 'using' or 'disclosing', in relation to personal data, includes using or disclosing the information contained in the data.

(3)   In determining for the purposes of this Act whether any information is recorded with the intention –

(a) that it should be processed by means of equipment operating automatically in response to instructions given for that purpose, or

(b) that it should form part of a relevant filing system,

it is immaterial that it is intended to be so processed or to form part of such a system only after being transferred to a country or territory outside the European Economic Area.

(4)   Where personal data are processed only for purposes for which they are required by or under any enactment to be processed, the person on whom the obligation to process the data is imposed by or under that enactment is for the purposes of this Act the data controller.

Sensitive personal data

2.   In this Act 'sensitive personal data' means personal data consisting of information as to –

(a) the racial or ethnic origin of the data subject,

(b) his political opinions,

(c) his religious beliefs or other beliefs of a similar nature,

(d) whether he is a member of a trade union (within the meaning of the *Trade Union and Labour Relations (Consolidation) Act 1992*),

(e) his physical or mental health or condition,

(f) his sexual life,

(g) the commission or alleged commission by him of any offence, or

(h) any proceedings for any offence committed or alleged to have been committed by him, the disposal of such proceedings or the sentence of any court in such proceedings.

The special purposes

3.   In this Act 'the special purposes' means any one or more of the following –
(a)   the purposes of journalism,
(b)   artistic purposes, and
(c)   literary purposes.

The data protection principles

4. – (1)   References in this Act to the data protection principles are to the principles set out in Part I of Schedule 1.

(2)   Those principles are to be interpreted in accordance with Part II of Schedule 1.

(3)   Schedule 2 (which applies to all personal data) and Schedule 3 (which applies only to sensitive personal data) set out conditions applying for the purposes of the first principle; and Schedule 4 sets out cases in which the eighth principle does not apply.

(4)   Subject to s27(1), it shall be the duty of a data controller to comply with the data protection principles in relation to all personal data with respect to which he is the data controller.

Application of Act

5. – (1)   Except as otherwise provided by or under s54, this Act applies to a data controller in respect of any data only if –
(a)   the data controller is established in the United Kingdom and the data are processed in the context of that establishment, or
(b)   the data controller is established neither in the United Kingdom nor in any other EEA State but uses equipment in the United Kingdom for processing the data otherwise than for the purposes of transit through the United Kingdom.

(2)   A data controller falling within subsection (1)(b) must nominate for the purposes of this Act a representative established in the United Kingdom.

(3)   For the purposes of subsections (1) and (2), each of the following is to be treated as established in the United Kingdom –

   (a)   an individual who is ordinarily resident in the United Kingdom,

   (b)   a body incorporated under the law of, or of any part of, the United Kingdom,

   (c)   a partnership or other unincorporated association formed under the law of any part of the United Kingdom, and

   (d)   any person who does not fall within paragraph (a), (b) or (c) but maintains in the United Kingdom –

      (i) an office, branch or agency through which he carries on any activity, or

      (ii) a regular practice;

   and the reference to establishment in any other EEA State has a corresponding meaning.

The Commissioner and the Tribunal

6. – (1)   The office originally established by s3(1)(a) of the Data Protection Act 1984 as the office of Data Protection Registrar shall continue to exist for the purposes of this Act but shall be known as the office of Data Protection Commissioner; and in this Act the Data Protection Commissioner is referred to as 'the Commissioner'.

(2)   The Commissioner shall be appointed by Her Majesty by Letters Patent.

(3)   For the purposes of this Act there shall continue to be a Data Protection Tribunal (in this Act referred to as 'the Tribunal').

(4)   The Tribunal shall consist of –

   (a)   a chairman appointed by the Lord Chancellor after consultation with the Lord Advocate,

   (b)   such number of deputy chairmen so appointed as the Lord Chancellor may determine, and

   (c)   such number of other members appointed by the Secretary of State as he may determine.

(5)   The members of the Tribunal appointed under subsec-
           tion (4)(a) and (b) shall be –
           (a) persons who have a seven-year general qualifica-
                tion, within the meaning of s71 of the *Courts and
                Legal Services Act 1990*,
           (b) advocates or solicitors in Scotland of at least seven
                years' standing, or
           (c) members of the bar of Northern Ireland or solici-
                tors of the Supreme Court of Northern Ireland of
                at least seven years' standing.

(6)   The members of the Tribunal appointed under subsec-
           tion (4)(c) shall be –
           (a) persons to represent the interests of data subjects,
                and
           (b) persons to represent the interests of data control-
                lers.

(7)   Schedule 5 has effect in relation to the Commissioner
           and the Tribunal.

Part II Rights of Data Subjects and Others

Right of access to personal data

7. – (1)   Subject to the following provisions of this section and to
           ss8 and 9, an individual is entitled –
           (a) to be informed by any data controller whether
                personal data of which that individual is the data
                subject are being processed by or on behalf of that
                data controller,
           (b) if that is the case, to be given by the data controller
                a description of –
                (i) the personal data of which that individual is
                the data subject,
                (ii) the purposes for which they are being or are to
                be processed, and
                (iii)the recipients or classes of recipients to whom
                they are or may be disclosed,
           (c) to have communicated to him in an intelligible
                form –
                (i) the information constituting any personal data
                of which that individual is the data subject, and

(ii) any information available to the data controller as to the source of those data, and

(d) where the processing by automatic means of personal data of which that individual is the data subject for the purpose of evaluating matters relating to him such as, for example, his performance at work, his creditworthiness, his reliability or his conduct, has constituted or is likely to constitute the sole basis for any decision significantly affecting him, to be informed by the data controller of the logic involved in that decision-taking.

(2)   A data controller is not obliged to supply any information under subsection (1) unless he has received –

(a) a request in writing, and

(b) except in prescribed cases, such fee (not exceeding the prescribed maximum) as he may require.

(3)   A data controller is not obliged to comply with a request under this section unless he is supplied with such information as he may reasonably require in order to satisfy himself as to the identity of the person making the request and to locate the information which that person seeks.

(4)   Where a data controller cannot comply with the request without disclosing information relating to another individual who can be identified from that information, he is not obliged to comply with the request unless –

(a) the other individual has consented to the disclosure of the information to the person making the request, or

(b) it is reasonable in all the circumstances to comply with the request without the consent of the other individual.

(5)   In subsection (4) the reference to information relating to another individual includes a reference to information identifying that individual as the source of the information sought by the request; and that subsection is not to be construed as excusing a data controller from communicating so much of the information

sought by the request as can be communicated without disclosing the identity of the other individual concerned, whether by the omission of names or other identifying particulars or otherwise.

(6)   In determining for the purposes of subsection (4)(b) whether it is reasonable in all the circumstances to comply with the request without the consent of the other individual concerned, regard shall be had, in particular, to –

(a)   any duty of confidentiality owed to the other individual,

(b)   any steps taken by the data controller with a view to seeking the consent of the other individual,

(c)   whether the other individual is capable of giving consent, and

(d)   any express refusal of consent by the other individual.

(7)   An individual making a request under this section may, in such cases as may be prescribed, specify that his request is limited to personal data of any prescribed description.

(8)   Subject to subsection (4), a data controller shall comply with a request under this section promptly and in any event before the end of the prescribed period beginning with the relevant day.

(9)   If a court is satisfied on the application of any person who has made a request under the foregoing provisions of this section that the data controller in question has failed to comply with the request in contravention of those provisions, the court may order him to comply with the request.

(10)   In this section –

'prescribed' means prescribed by the Secretary of State by regulations;

'the prescribed maximum' means such amount as may be prescribed;

'the prescribed period' means 40 days or such other period as may be prescribed;

'the relevant day', in relation to a request under this section, means the day on which the data controller receives the request or, if later, the first day on which the data controller has both the required fee and the information referred to in subsection (3).

(11)   Different amounts or periods may be prescribed under this section in relation to different cases.

Provisions supplementary to s7.

8. – (1)   The Secretary of State may by regulations provide that, in such cases as may be prescribed, a request for information under any provision of subsection (1) of s7 is to be treated as extending also to information under other provisions of that subsection.

(2)   The obligation imposed by s7(1)(c)(i) must be complied with by supplying the data subject with a copy of the information in permanent form unless –

(a)   the supply of such a copy is not possible or would involve disproportionate effort, or

(b)   the data subject agrees otherwise;

and where any of the information referred to in s7(1)(c)(i) is expressed in terms which are not intelligible without explanation the copy must be accompanied by an explanation of those terms.

(3)   Where a data controller has previously complied with a request made under s7 by an individual, the data controller is not obliged to comply with a subsequent identical or similar request under that section by that individual unless a reasonable interval has elapsed between compliance with the previous request and the making of the current request.

(4)   In determining for the purposes of subsection (3) whether requests under s7 are made at reasonable intervals, regard shall be had to the nature of the data, the purpose for which the data are processed and the frequency with which the data are altered.

(5)   Section 7(1)(d) is not to be regarded as requiring the provision of information as to the logic involved in any decision-taking if, and to the extent that, the information constitutes a trade secret.

(6)   The information to be supplied pursuant to a request under s7 must be supplied by reference to the data in question at the time when the request is received, except that it may take account of any amendment or deletion made between that time and the time when the information is supplied, being an amendment or deletion that would have been made regardless of the receipt of the request.

(7)   For the purposes of s7(4) and (5) another individual can be identified from the information being disclosed if he can be identified from that information, or from that and any other information which, in the reasonable belief of the data controller, is likely to be in, or to come into, the possession of the data subject making the request.

Application of s7 where data controller is credit reference agency

9. – (1)   Where the data controller is a credit reference agency, s7 has effect subject to the provisions of this section.

(2)   An individual making a request under s7 may limit his request to personal data relevant to his financial standing, and shall be taken to have so limited his request unless the request shows a contrary intention.

(3)   Where the data controller receives a request under s7 in a case where personal data of which the individual making the request is the data subject are being processed by or on behalf of the data controller, the obligation to supply information under that section includes an obligation to give the individual making the request a statement, in such form as may be prescribed by the Secretary of State by regulations, of the individual's rights –

(a)   under s159 of the *Consumer Credit Act 1974*, and

(b)   to the extent required by the prescribed form, under this Act.

Right to prevent processing likely to cause damage or distress

10. – (1)   Subject to subsection (2), an individual is entitled at any time by notice in writing to a data controller to require the data controller at the end of such period as is reasonable in the circumstances to cease, or not to begin, processing, or processing for a specified purpose or in a specified manner, any personal data in respect of which he is the data subject, on the ground that, for specified reasons –

(a) the processing of those data or their processing for that purpose or in that manner is causing or is likely to cause substantial damage or substantial distress to him or to another, and

(b) that damage or distress is or would be unwarranted.

(2)   Subsection (1) does not apply –

(a) in a case where any of the conditions in paragraphs 1 to 4 of Schedule 2 is met, or

(b) in such other cases as may be prescribed by the Secretary of State by order.

(3)   The data controller must within 21 days of receiving a notice under subsection (1) ('the data subject notice') give the individual who gave it a written notice –

(a) stating that he has complied or intends to comply with the data subject notice, or

(b) stating his reasons for regarding the data subject notice as to any extent unjustified and the extent (if any) to which he has complied or intends to comply with it.

(4)   If a court is satisfied, on the application of any person who has given a notice under subsection (1) which appears to the court to be justified (or to be justified to any extent), that the data controller in question has failed to comply with the notice, the court may order him to take such steps for complying with the notice (or for complying with it to that extent) as the court thinks fit.

(5)   The failure by a data subject to exercise the right conferred by subsection (1) or section 11(1) does not affect any other right conferred on him by this Part.

Right to prevent processing for purposes of direct marketing

11. – (1)   An individual is entitled at any time by notice in writing to a data controller to require the data controller at the end of such period as is reasonable in the circumstances to cease, or not to begin, processing for the purposes of direct marketing personal data in respect of which he is the data subject.

(2)   If the court is satisfied, on the application of any person who has given a notice under subsection (1), that the data controller has failed to comply with the notice, the court may order him to take such steps for complying with the notice as the court thinks fit.

(3)   In this section 'direct marketing' means the communication (by whatever means) of any advertising or marketing material which is directed to particular individuals.

Rights in relation to automated decision-taking

12. – (1)   An individual is entitled at any time, by notice in writing to any data controller, to require the data controller to ensure that no decision taken by or on behalf of the data controller which significantly affects that individual is based solely on the processing by automatic means of personal data in respect of which that individual is the data subject for the purpose of evaluating matters relating to him such as, for example, his performance at work, his creditworthiness, his reliability or his conduct.

(2)   Where, in a case where no notice under subsection (1) has effect, a decision which significantly affects an individual is based solely on such processing as is mentioned in subsection (1) –

(a)   the data controller must as soon as reasonably practicable notify the individual that the decision was taken on that basis, and

(b)   the individual is entitled, within 21 days of receiving that notification from the data controller, by notice in writing to require the data controller to reconsider the decision or to take a new decision otherwise than on that basis.

(3)   The data controller must, within 21 days of receiving a notice under subsection (2)(b) ('the data subject notice') give the individual a written notice specifying the steps that he intends to take to comply with the data subject notice.

(4)   A notice under subsection (1) does not have effect in relation to an exempt decision; and nothing in subsection (2) applies to an exempt decision.

(5)   In subsection (4) 'exempt decision' means any decision –
   (a)   in respect of which the condition in subsection (6) and the condition in subsection (7) are met, or
   (b)   which is made in such other circumstances as may be prescribed by the Secretary of State by order.

(6)   The condition in this subsection is that the decision-
   (a)   is taken in the course of steps taken –
      (i)   for the purpose of considering whether to enter into a contract with the data subject,
      (ii)   with a view to entering into such a contract, or
      (iii)   in the course of performing such a contract, or
   (b)   is authorised or required by or under any enactment.

(7)   The condition in this subsection is that either –
   (a)   the effect of the decision is to grant a request of the data subject, or
   (b)   steps have been taken to safeguard the legitimate interests of the data subject (for example, by allowing him to make representations).

(8)   If a court is satisfied on the application of a data subject that a person taking a decision in respect of him ('the responsible person') has failed to comply with subsection (1) or (2)(b), the court may order the responsible person to reconsider the decision, or to take a new decision which is not based solely on such processing as is mentioned in subsection (1).

(9)   An order under subsection (8) shall not affect the rights of any person other than the data subject and the responsible person.

Compensation for failure to comply with certain requirements

13. – (1)   An individual who suffers damage by reason of any contravention by a data controller of any of the requirements of this Act is entitled to compensation from the data controller for that damage.

(2)   An individual who suffers distress by reason of any contravention by a data controller of any of the requirements of this Act is entitled to compensation from the data controller for that distress if –

    (a)   the individual also suffers damage by reason of the contravention, or

    (b)   the contravention relates to the processing of personal data for the special purposes.

(3)   In proceedings brought against a person by virtue of this section it is a defence to prove that he had taken such care as in all the circumstances was reasonably required to comply with the requirement concerned. Rectification, blocking, erasure and destruction.

14. – (1)   If a court is satisfied on the application of a data subject that personal data of which the applicant is the subject are inaccurate, the court may order the data controller to rectify, block, erase or destroy those data and any other personal data in respect of which he is the data controller and which contain an expression of opinion which appears to the court to be based on the inaccurate data.

(2)   Subsection (1) applies whether or not the data accurately record information received or obtained by the data controller from the data subject or a third party but where the data accurately record such information, then –

    (a)   if the requirements mentioned in paragraph 7 of Part II of Schedule 1 have been complied with, the court may, instead of making an order under subsection (1), make an order requiring the data to be supplemented by such statement of the true facts relating to the matters dealt with by the data as the court may approve, and

(b) if all or any of those requirements have not been complied with, the court may, instead of making an order under that subsection, make such order as it thinks fit for securing compliance with those requirements with or without a further order requiring the data to be supplemented by such a statement as is mentioned in paragraph (a).

(3)   Where the court –

(a) makes an order under subsection (1), or

(b) is satisfied on the application of a data subject that personal data of which he was the data subject and which have been rectified, blocked, erased or destroyed were inaccurate,

it may, where it considers it reasonably practicable, order the data controller to notify third parties to whom the data have been disclosed of the rectification, blocking, erasure or destruction.

(4)   If a court is satisfied on the application of a data subject –

(a) that he has suffered damage by reason of any contravention by a data controller of any of the requirements of this Act in respect of any personal data, in circumstances entitling him to compensation under s13, and

(b) that there is a substantial risk of further contravention in respect of those data in such circumstances,

the court may order the rectification, blocking, erasure or destruction of any of those data.

(5)   Where the court makes an order under subsection (4) it may, where it considers it reasonably practicable, order the data controller to notify third parties to whom the data have been disclosed of the rectification, blocking, erasure or destruction.

(6)   In determining whether it is reasonably practicable to require such notification as is mentioned in subsection

(3) or (5) the court shall have regard, in particular, to the number of persons who would have to be notified.

Jurisdiction and procedure

15. – (1)   The jurisdiction conferred by ss7 to 14 is exercisable by the High Court or a county court or, in Scotland, by the Court of Session or the sheriff.

(2)   For the purpose of determining any question whether an applicant under subsection (9) of s7 is entitled to the information which he seeks (including any question whether any relevant data are exempt from that section by virtue of Part IV) a court may require the information constituting any data processed by or on behalf of the data controller and any information as to the logic involved in any decision-taking as mentioned in s7(1)(d) to be made available for its own inspection but shall not, pending the determination of that question in the applicant's favour, require the information sought by the applicant to be disclosed to him or his representatives whether by discovery (or, in Scotland, recovery) or otherwise.

Part IV Exemptions

Health, education and social work

30. – (1)   The Secretary of State may by order exempt from the subject information provisions, or modify those provisions in relation to, personal data consisting of information as to the physical or mental health or condition of the data subject.

(2)   The Secretary of State may by order exempt from the subject information provisions, or modify those provisions in relation to –

(a)   personal data in respect of which the data controller is the proprietor of, or a teacher at, a school, and which consist of information relating to persons who are or have been pupils at the school, or

(b)   personal data in respect of which the data controller is an education authority in Scotland, and which consist of information relating to persons who are receiving, or have received, further education provided by the authority.

(3)   The Secretary of State may by order exempt from the subject information provisions, or modify those provisions in relation to, personal data of such other descriptions as may be specified in the order, being information –

(a)   processed by government departments or local authorities or by voluntary organisations or other bodies designated by or under the order, and

(b)   appearing to him to be processed in the course of, or for the purposes of, carrying out social work in relation to the data subject or other individuals;

but the Secretary of State shall not under this subsection confer any exemption or make any modification except so far as he considers that the application to the data of those provisions (or of those provisions without modification) would be likely to prejudice the carrying out of social work.

(4)   An order under this section may make different provision in relation to data consisting of information of different descriptions.

(5)   In this section –

'education authority' and 'further education' have the same meaning as in the Education (Scotland) Act 1980 ('the 1980 Act'), and

'proprietor' –

(a)   in relation to a school in England or Wales, has the same meaning as in the Education Act 1996,

(b)   in relation to a school in Scotland, means –

(i)   in the case of a self-governing school, the board of management within the meaning of the Self-Governing Schools etc (Scotland) Act 1989,

(ii)   in the case of an independent school, the proprietor within the meaning of the 1980 Act,

(iii)   in the case of a grant-aided school, the managers within the meaning of the 1980 Act, and

       (iv) in the case of a public school, the education authority within the meaning of the 1980 Act, and

  (c) in relation to a school in Northern Ireland, has the same meaning as in the Education and Libraries (Northern Ireland) Order 1986 and includes, in the case of a controlled school, the Board of Governors of the school.

Powers to make further exemptions by order

38. – (1) The Secretary of State may by order exempt from the subject information provisions personal data consisting of information the disclosure of which is prohibited or restricted by or under any enactment if and to the extent that he considers it necessary for the safeguarding of the interests of the data subject or the rights and freedoms of any other individual that the prohibition or restriction ought to prevail over those provisions.

(2) The Secretary of State may by order exempt from the non-disclosure provisions any disclosures of personal data made in circumstances specified in the order, if he considers the exemption is necessary for the safeguarding of the interests of the data subject or the rights and freedoms of any other individual.

General

Meaning of 'health professional'

69. – (1) In this Act 'health professional' means any of the following –

  (a) a registered medical practitioner,

  (b) a registered dentist as defined by s53(1) of the Dentists Act 1984,

  (c) a registered optician as defined by s36(1) of the Opticians Act 1989,

  (d) a registered pharmaceutical chemist as defined by s24(1) of the Pharmacy Act 1954 or a registered person as defined by Article 2(2) of the Pharmacy (Northern Ireland) Order 1976,

  (e) a registered nurse, midwife or health visitor,

(f) a registered osteopath as defined by s41 of the
     Osteopaths Act 1993,

(g) a registered chiropractor as defined by s43 of the
     Chiropractors Act 1994,

(h) any person who is registered as a member of a
     profession to which the Professions Supplemen-
     tary to Medicine Act 1960 for the time being
     extends,

(i) a clinical psychologist, child psychotherapist or
     speech therapist,

(j) a music therapist employed by a health service
     body, and

(k) a scientist employed by such a body as head of a
     department.

(2) In subsection (1)(a) 'registered medical practitioner'
     includes any person who is provisionally registered
     under s15 or 21 of the Medical Act 1983 and is engaged
     in such employment as is mentioned in subsection (3)
     of that section.

(3) In subsection (1) 'health service body' means –

(a) a Health Authority established under s8 of the
     National Health Service Act 1977,

(b) a Special Health Authority established under s11
     of that Act,

(c) a Health Board within the meaning of the
     National Health Service (Scotland) Act 1978,

(d) a Special Health Board within the meaning of that
     Act,

(e) the managers of a State Hospital provided under
     s102 of that Act,

(f) a National Health Service trust first established
     under s5 of the National Health Service and Com-
     munity Care Act 1990 or s12A of the National
     Health Service (Scotland) Act 1978,

(g) a Health and Social Services Board established
     under Article 16 of the Health and Personal Social
     Services (Northern Ireland) Order 1972,

(h) a special health and social services agency estab-
     lished under the Health and Personal Social Ser-

vices (Special Agencies) (Northern Ireland) Order 1990, or

(i) a Health and Social Services trust established under Article 10 of the Health and Personal Social Services (Northern Ireland) Order 1991.

Supplementary definitions

70. – (1) In this Act, unless the context otherwise requires –

'business' includes any trade or profession;

'the Commissioner' means the Data Protection Commissioner;

'credit reference agency' has the same meaning as in the Consumer Credit Act 1974;

'the Data Protection Directive' means Directive 95/46/EC on the protection of individuals with regard to the processing of personal data and on the free movement of such data;

'EEA State' means a State which is a contracting party to the Agreement on the European Economic Area signed at Oporto on 2 May 1992 as adjusted by the Protocol signed at Brussels on 17 March 1993;

'enactment' includes an enactment passed after this Act;

'government department' includes a Northern Ireland department and any body or authority exercising statutory functions on behalf of the Crown;

'Minister of the Crown' has the same meaning as in the Ministers of the Crown Act 1975;

'public register' means any register which pursuant to a requirement imposed –

(a) by or under any enactment, or

(b) in pursuance of any international agreement,

is open to public inspection or open to inspection by any person having a legitimate interest;

'pupil' –

(a) in relation to a school in England and Wales, means a registered pupil within the meaning of the Education Act 1996,

(b)   in relation to a school in Scotland, means a pupil within the meaning of the Education (Scotland) Act 1980, and

(c)   in relation to a school in Northern Ireland, means a registered pupil within the meaning of the Education and Libraries (Northern Ireland) Order 1986;

'recipient', in relation to any personal data, means any person to whom the data are disclosed, including any person (such as an employee or agent of the data controller, a data processor or an employee or agent of a data processor) to whom they are disclosed in the course of processing the data for the data controller, but does not include any person to whom disclosure is or may be made as a result of, or with a view to, a particular inquiry by or on behalf of that person made in the exercise of any power conferred by law;

'registered company' means a company registered under the enactments relating to companies for the time being in force in the United Kingdom;

'school' –

(a)   in relation to England and Wales, has the same meaning as in the Education Act 1996,

(b)   in relation to Scotland, has the same meaning as in the Education (Scotland) Act 1980, and

(c)   in relation to Northern Ireland, has the same meaning as in the Education and Libraries (Northern Ireland) Order 1986;

'teacher' includes –

(a)   in Great Britain, head teacher, and

(b)   in Northern Ireland, the principal of a school;

'third party', in relation to personal data, means any person other than –

(a)   the data subject,

(b)   the data controller, or

(c)   any data processor or other person authorised to process data for the data controller or processor;

'the Tribunal' means the Data Protection Tribunal.

(2)   For the purposes of this Act data are inaccurate if they are incorrect or misleading as to any matter of fact.

Schedule 1

The Data Protection Principles

Part I

The Principles

1.   Personal data shall be processed fairly and lawfully and, in particular, shall not be processed unless –
   (a)   at least one of the conditions in Schedule 2 is met, and
   (b)   in the case of sensitive personal data, at least one of the conditions in Schedule 3 is also met.

2.   Personal data shall be obtained only for one or more specified and lawful purposes, and shall not be further processed in any manner incompatible with that purpose or those purposes.

3.   Personal data shall be adequate, relevant and not excessive in relation to the purpose or purposes for which they are processed.

4.   Personal data shall be accurate and, where necessary, kept up to date.

5.   Personal data processed for any purpose or purposes shall not be kept for longer than is necessary for that purpose or those purposes.

6.   Personal data shall be processed in accordance with the rights of data subjects under this Act.

7.   Appropriate technical and organisational measures shall be taken against unauthorised or unlawful processing of personal data and against accidental loss or destruction of, or damage to, personal data.

8.   Personal data shall not be transferred to a country or territory outside the European Economic Area unless that country or territory ensures an adequate level of protection for the rights and freedoms of data subjects in relation to the processing of personal data.

Part II

Interpretation of the Principles in Part I

The first principle

1. – (1)   In determining for the purposes of the first principle whether personal data are processed fairly, regard is to be had to the method by which they are obtained, including in particular whether any person from whom they are obtained is deceived or misled as to the purpose or purposes for which they are to be processed.

(2)   Subject to paragraph 2, for the purposes of the first principle data are to be treated as obtained fairly if they consist of information obtained from a person who –

    (a)   is authorised by or under any enactment to supply it, or

    (b)   is required to supply it by or under any enactment or by any convention or other instrument imposing an international obligation on the United Kingdom.

2. – (1)   Subject to paragraph 3, for the purposes of the first principle personal data are not to be treated as processed fairly unless –

    (a)   in the case of data obtained from the data subject, the data controller ensures so far as practicable that the data subject has, is provided with, or has made readily available to him, the information specified in sub-paragraph (3), and

    (b)   in any other case, the data controller ensures so far as practicable that, before the relevant time or as soon as practicable after that time, the data subject has, is provided with, or has made readily available to him, the information specified in sub-paragraph (3).

(2)   In sub-paragraph (1)(b) 'the relevant time' means –

    (a)   the time when the data controller first processes the data, or

    (b)   in a case where at that time disclosure to a third party within a reasonable period is envisaged –

(i) if the data are in fact disclosed to such a person within that period, the time when the data are first disclosed,

(ii) if within that period the data controller becomes, or ought to become, aware that the data are unlikely to be disclosed to such a person within that period, the time when the data controller does become, or ought to become, so aware, or

(iii) in any other case, the end of that period.

(3)   The information referred to in sub-paragraph (1) is as follows, namely –

(a) the identity of the data controller,

(b) if he has nominated a representative for the purposes of this Act, the identity of that representative,

(c) the purpose or purposes for which the data are intended to be processed, and

(d) any further information which is necessary, having regard to the specific circumstances in which the data are or are to be processed, to enable processing in respect of the data subject to be fair.

3. – (1)   Paragraph 2(1)(b) does not apply where either of the primary conditions in sub-paragraph (2), together with such further conditions as may be prescribed by the Secretary of State by order, are met.

(2)   The primary conditions referred to in sub-paragraph (1) are –

(a) that the provision of that information would involve a disproportionate effort, or

(b) that the recording of the information to be contained in the data by, or the disclosure of the data by, the data controller is necessary for compliance with any legal obligation to which the data controller is subject, other than an obligation imposed by contract.

4. – (1)   Personal data which contain a general identifier falling within a description prescribed by the Secretary of

State by order are not to be treated as processed fairly and lawfully unless they are processed in compliance with any conditions so prescribed in relation to general identifiers of that description.

(2)   In sub-paragraph (1) 'a general identifier' means any identifier (such as, for example, a number or code used for identification purposes) which –

(a)   relates to an individual, and

(b)   forms part of a set of similar identifiers which is of general application.

The second principle

5.   The purpose or purposes for which personal data are obtained may in particular be specified –

(a)   in a notice given for the purposes of paragraph 2 by the data controller to the data subject, or

(b)   in a notification given to the Commissioner under Part III of this Act.

6.   In determining whether any disclosure of personal data is compatible with the purpose or purposes for which the data were obtained, regard is to be had to the purpose or purposes for which the personal data are intended to be processed by any person to whom they are disclosed.

The fourth principle

7.   The fourth principle is not to be regarded as being contravened by reason of any inaccuracy in personal data which accurately record information obtained by the data controller from the data subject or a third party in a case where –

(a)   having regard to the purpose or purposes for which the data were obtained and further processed, the data controller has taken reasonable steps to ensure the accuracy of the data, and

(b)   if the data subject has notified the data controller of the data subject's view that the data are inaccurate, the data indicate that fact.

The sixth principle

8.   A person is to be regarded as contravening the sixth
        principle if, but only if –
        (a)   he contravenes s7 by failing to supply information
              in accordance with that section,
        (b)   he contravenes s10 by failing to comply with a
              notice given under subsection (1) of that section to
              the extent that the notice is justified or by failing to
              give a notice under subsection (3) of that section,
        (c)   he contravenes s11 by failing to comply with a
              notice given under subsection (1) of that section,
              or
        (d)   he contravenes s12 by failing to comply with a
              notice given under subsection (1) or (2)(b) of that
              section or by failing to give a notification under
              subsection (2)(a) of that section or a notice under
              subsection (3) of that section.

The seventh principle

9.   Having regard to the state of technological develop-
        ment and the cost of implementing any measures, the
        measures must ensure a level of security appropriate
        to –
        (a)   the harm that might result from such unauthor-
              ised or unlawful processing or accidental loss,
              destruction or damage as are mentioned in the
              seventh principle, and
        (b)   the nature of the data to be protected.

10.   The data controller must take reasonable steps to
        ensure the reliability of any employees of his who have
        access to the personal data.

11.   Where processing of personal data is carried out by a
        data processor on behalf of a data controller, the data
        controller must in order to comply with the seventh
        principle –
        (a)   choose a data processor providing sufficient guar-
              antees in respect of the technical and organisa-
              tional security measures governing the processing
              to be carried out, and

(b)   take reasonable steps to ensure compliance with those measures.

12.   Where processing of personal data is carried out by a data processor on behalf of a data controller, the data controller is not to be regarded as complying with the seventh principle unless –
  (a)   the processing is carried out under a contract –
    (i)   which is made or evidenced in writing, and
    (ii) under which the data processor is to act only on instructions from the data controller, and
  (b)   the contract requires the data processor to comply with obligations equivalent to those imposed on a data controller by the seventh principle.

The eighth principle

13.   An adequate level of protection is one which is adequate in all the circumstances of the case, having regard in particular to –
  (a)   the nature of the personal data,
  (b)   the country or territory of origin of the information contained in the data,
  (c)   the country or territory of final destination of that information,
  (d)   the purposes for which and period during which the data are intended to be processed,
  (e)   the law in force in the country or territory in question,
  (f)   the international obligations of that country or territory,
  (g)   any relevant codes of conduct or other rules which are enforceable in that country or territory (whether generally or by arrangement in particular cases), and
  (h)   any security measures taken in respect of the data in that country or territory.

14.   The eighth principle does not apply to a transfer falling within any paragraph of Schedule 4, except in such circumstances and to such extent as the Secretary of State may by order provide.

15. – (1)   Where –

    (a)   in any proceedings under this Act any question arises as to whether the requirement of the eighth principle as to an adequate level of protection is met in relation to the transfer of any personal data to a country or territory outside the European Economic Area, and

    (b)   a Community finding has been made in relation to transfers of the kind in question,

    that question is to be determined in accordance with that finding.

(2)   In sub-paragraph (1) 'Community finding' means a finding of the European Commission, under the procedure provided for in Article 31(2) of the Data Protection Directive, that a country or territory outside the European Economic Area does, or does not, ensure an adequate level of protection within the meaning of Article 25(2) of the Directive.

Schedule 2

Conditions Relevant for Purposes of the First Principle Processing of any Personal Data

1.   The data subject has given his consent to the processing.

2.   The processing is necessary –

    (a)   for the performance of a contract to which the data subject is a party, or

    (b)   for the taking of steps at the request of the data subject with a view to entering into a contract.

3.   The processing is necessary for compliance with any legal obligation to which the data controller is subject, other than an obligation imposed by contract.

4.   The processing is necessary in order to protect the vital interests of the data subject.

5.   The processing is necessary –

    (a)   for the administration of justice,

    (b)   for the exercise of any functions conferred on any person by or under any enactment,

(c)   for the exercise of any functions of the Crown, a
Minister of the Crown or a government department, or

(d)   for the exercise of any other functions of a public
nature exercised in the public interest by any
person.

6. – (1)   The processing is necessary for the purposes of legitimate interests pursued by the data controller or by the
third party or parties to whom the data are disclosed,
except where the processing is unwarranted in any
particular case by reason of prejudice to the rights and
freedoms or legitimate interests of the data subject.

(2)   The Secretary of State may by order specify particular
circumstances in which this condition is, or is not, to be
taken to be satisfied.

Schedule 3

Conditions Relevant for Purposes of the First Principle
Processing of Sensitive Personal Data

1.   The data subject has given his explicit consent to the
processing of the personal data.

2. – (1)   The processing is necessary for the purposes of exercising or performing any right or obligation which is conferred or imposed by law on the data controller in
connection with employment.

(2)   The Secretary of State may by order –

(a)   exclude the application of sub-paragraph (1) in
such cases as may be specified, or

(b)   provide that, in such cases as may be specified, the
condition in sub-paragraph (1) is not to be
regarded as satisfied unless such further conditions as may be specified in the order are also satisfied.

3.   The processing is necessary –

(a)   in order to protect the vital interests of the data
subject or another person, in a case where –

(i)   consent cannot be given by or on behalf of the
data subject, or

(ii) the data controller cannot reasonably be expected to obtain the consent of the data subject, or

(b) in order to protect the vital interests of another person, in a case where consent by or on behalf of the data subject has been unreasonably withheld.

4.   The processing –

(a) is carried out in the course of its legitimate activities by any body or association which –

(i)   is not established or conducted for profit, and

(ii) exists for political, philosophical, religious or trade-union purposes,

(b) is carried out with appropriate safeguards for the rights and freedoms of data subjects,

(c) relates only to individuals who either are members of the body or association or have regular contact with it in connection with its purposes, and

(d) does not involve disclosure of the personal data to a third party without the consent of the data subject.

5.   The information contained in the personal data has been made public as a result of steps deliberately taken by the data subject.

6.   The processing –

(a) is necessary for the purpose of, or in connection with, any legal proceedings (including prospective legal proceedings),

(b) is necessary for the purpose of obtaining legal advice, or

(c) is otherwise necessary for the purposes of establishing, exercising or defending legal rights.

7. – (1)   The processing is necessary –

(a) for the administration of justice,

(b) for the exercise of any functions conferred on any person by or under an enactment, or

(c)   for the exercise of any functions of the Crown, a Minister of the Crown or a government department.

(2)   The Secretary of State may by order –

(a)   exclude the application of sub-paragraph (1) in such cases as may be specified, or

(b)   provide that, in such cases as may be specified, the condition in sub-paragraph (1) is not to be regarded as satisfied unless such further conditions as may be specified in the order are also satisfied.

8. – (1)   The processing is necessary for medical purposes and is undertaken by –

(a)   a health professional, or

(b)   a person who in the circumstances owes a duty of confidentiality which is equivalent to that which would arise if that person were a health professional.

(2)   In this paragraph 'medical purposes' includes the purposes of preventative medicine, medical diagnosis, medical research, the provision of care and treatment and the management of healthcare services.

9. – (1)   The processing –

(a)   is of sensitive personal data consisting of information as to racial or ethnic origin,

(b)   is necessary for the purpose of identifying or keeping under review the existence or absence of equality of opportunity or treatment between persons of different racial or ethnic origins, with a view to enabling such equality to be promoted or maintained, and

(c)   is carried out with appropriate safeguards for the rights and freedoms of data subjects.

(2)   The Secretary of State may by order specify circumstances in which processing falling within sub-paragraph (1)(a) and (b) is, or is not, to be taken for the purposes of sub-paragraph (1)(c) to be carried out with

appropriate safeguards for the rights and freedoms of data subjects.

10.   The personal data are processed in circumstances specified in an order made by the Secretary of State for the purposes of this paragraph.

Appendix 7:
Useful Addresses

British Medical Association, BMA House, Tavistock Square, London WC1H 9JP. Telephone 020 7387 4499.

British Dental Association, 64 Wimpole Street, London W1M 8AL. Telephone 020 7935 0875.

Chartered Society of Physiotherapy, Professional Affairs Department, 14 Bedford Row, London WC1R 4ED. Telephone 020 7306 6666.

Department of Health, Richmond House, 79 Whitehall, London SW1A 2NS. Telephone 020 7210 3000.

General Council and Register of Osteopaths, 56 London Street, Reading, Berkshire RG1 4SQ. Telephone 01734 576585.

General Medical Council, 178-202 Great Portland Street, London W1N 6JE. Telephone 020 7580 7642.

General Dental Council, 37 Wimpole Street, London W1M 8DQ. Telephone 020 7887 3800.

Royal College of Veterinary Surgeons, Professional Conduct Department, Belgravia House, 62-64 Horseferry Road, London SW1P 2AF. Telephone 020 7222 2001.

United Kingdom Central Council for Nursing, Midwifery and Health Visiting, 23 Portland Place, London W1N 4JT. Telephone 020 7637 7181.

Index

A-G v Guardian [1987] 5n
A-G v Guardian Newspapers Ltd
  (No 2) [1990] 19-20, 77
A-G v Jonathan Cape Ltd [1976] . 5n, 7n
A-G v Times Newspapers Ltd [1976]. . 5n
abortion 23-4
Abortion Regulations 1991 23-4
abuse 88, 106
access
  health records . . 56-62, 88-9, 100-1
  personal data 44, 115-19
Access to Health Records Act
  1990 . . . . 31, 57, 61, 88-9, 96, 100
Access to Medical Reports Act
  1988 59-60
account of profits 65
accountability 97, 99
accuracy of data. 123-4, 134
Addis v Gramophone Co [1909] . . . 67n
AIDS 9, 10, 50
American Cyanamid v Ethicon
  [1975] 63, 64
Andersson (Anne-Marie) v Sweden
  [1998] 50n, 53
anonymised information 6, 103
appeal
  Human Rights Act 1998 47
  see also Court of Appeal
Appleton v Garrett [1997] 69n
Argyll v Argyll [1967]. 4n, 7n
attendance confidentiality 102
audit. 89, 101, 103
automated decision-taking. . 44, 121-3

balance of convenience 64
births. 25
Bolam test 19

British Steel Corporation v Granada
  Television Ltd [1981] 70
Broome v Cassell & Co [1972] 69n
BSC v Granada Television Ltd [1981]. 4n
Buckley v UK [1996] 48n

Chartered Society of
  Physiotherapists 102-6
children 16-18
Children Act 1989 106
Chiropractors Act 1994 130
Church of Scientology v DHSS
  [1979] 33n
circumstances of confidentiality . . 6-8
Civil Procedure Rules
  (CPR) . . 29, 30n, 31, 32-4, 38-9, 55
Coco v AN Clark (Engineering) Ltd
  [1969] 20n
Code of Professional Conduct
  (UKCC) 97-8
common law
  obligation to keep
    confidences. 2-22, 23
  public interest immunity. 39
  rights of access to health
    records. 56-7
  statute influence 23
communicable diseases 92-4
  see also infectious diseases
compensation 44, 47-8, 123-5
  see also damages
Computer Misuse Act 1990 . . . 100-1
computer-held records . 95, 96, 100-1
consent
  Chartered Society of
    Physiotherapists guidelines . 103
  children 16, 17, 18

Data Protection Act
  1998 . . . . 116, 117, 137, 138-9
disclosure during or anticipating
  litigation 29
disclosure regarding sexually
  transmitted diseases 25
disclosure without 87-9
GMC guidelines 15, 85, 86, 87-8, 90
medical reports. 60
patients with mental
  disorder 18-19
Royal College of Veterinary
  Surgeons guidelines 110
sensitive personal data
  processing 43
third party access to health
  records. 61-2
UKCC guidelines 98
constructive trusts 66
Consumer Credit Act 1974 . . 119, 129
contract
  automated decision-taking . . . 122
  damages for breach of . . . 66, 67-8
  data processing 136, 137
  employment 100, 101
  language of 1
  obligation to keep confidences . 2-3
Conway v Rimmer [1968] 35n
Copp v Chief Constable of Avon and
  Somerset Police [1997]. 37n
Copyright, Designs and Patents
  Act 1988 69
County Courts Act
  1984 . . . . 30n, 33, 79, 80
Court of Appeal . 6, 11-12, 36-7, 52, 57
Courts and Legal Services Act
  1990 115
credit reference agencies. 119
crime 11-12, 26-7, 90, 106
Criminal Procedure (Attendance
  of Witnesses) Act 1965 27
Crossman diaries 5-6

D v NSPCC [1977] 35
damages . . . 47-8, 64, 65, 66-9, 73, 80
  see also compensation
data controller
  . . . . 41, 43, 44-5, 111, 112, 113
  automated decision-taking . . 121-3
  credit reference agencies 119

data protection
  principles . . . 132-3, 134, 135-6
  definition 110
  exemptions 125-7
  failure to comply with certain
    requirements. 125-7
  legal obligation 137
  legitimate interests 138
  prevention of data processing
    likely to cause damage or
    distress 119-20
  prevention of data processing
    for purposes of direct
    marketing 121
  right of access to data . . 58, 115-19
data definition 110
data processor . 41, 42, 43, 110, 135-6
Data Protection Act 1984 . . 40, 57, 61
  (Access Modification) (Health)
    Order 1987. 100
  Data Protection Registrar. . . . 114
  GDC guidelines 96
  Royal College of Veterinary
    Surgeons guidelines 108
Data Protection Act 1998
  (DPA) 21, 40-5, 110-41
  case study 72-3, 75, 79
  patient's rights of access to
    health records 58-9, 61
  Royal College of Veterinary
    Surgeons guidelines 107
Data Protection
  Commissioner 41, 44-5, 114
Data Protection Directive
  (EC) 40, 41, 129, 137
data protection principles . 113, 131-7
Data Protection (Subject Access
  Modification) (Health) Order
  2000 . . . . 58, 61
Data Protection Tribunal. . . . 114-15
data subject . 41, 43, 45, 122, 132, 139
  access to personal data 58
  compensation. 123-5
  data processing. . . . 120, 137, 138
  definition 111
  exemptions 127
  rights 115-25
death of patients 3, 15, 61, 88-9
declarations 69
defamation 3, 20, 68
delivery up orders. 66

dentists 95-6, 127
Dentists Act 1984. 127
destruction orders. 66
detriment. 19-21
direct marketing 44, 121
disability, persons under a. . . . 18-19
disclosure of confidential information
    abortion 24
    after death of patient . . 3, 15, 88-9
    compulsory under statute 23
    in connection with judicial or
        other statutory proceedings. 90-1
    crime 27
    Data Protection Act 1998   72-3,
        111-12, 116, 127, 130, 139
    data protection
        principles 132-3, 134
    detriment. 20, 21
    doctor's fiduciary
        responsibility 6, 66
    European Court of Human
        Rights 50, 52, 53
    Freedom of Information Bill . . 59
    GMC guidelines 85-92
    health records 27-8, 61-2
    inspectors of taxes 90-1
    in the interests of others . . . 89-90
    legal effects of 69
    medical reports. 60
    minors 18
    negligent 21
    in patient's medical interests. . 87-8
    permissible under statute 23
    prohibition. 4
    public interest 3, 8-12, 34-9
    research 15, 89
    Royal College of Veterinary
        Surgeons guidelines . 107-8, 109
    serious communicable
        diseases 92-3
    sexually transmitted diseases . . 25
    third party access to health
        records. 61-2
    UKCC guidelines 98-9
    unconscionable
        behaviour 8, 13-14
    where litigation is contemplated
        or proceeding 29-39
    within teams 86-7, 104
    without consent 87-9
disposal of patient records 96

distress
    compensation from data
        controller. 123
    damages for 67, 68
    prevention of data processing
        likely to cause. 44, 119-20
doctor-patient
    relationship 5, 7-8, 22, 60, 66
doctors
    fiduciary responsibility 6, 66
    fitness to practice. 90
    GMC guidelines 14
    GPnet. 43
    medical reports. 60
    need for confidentiality 1
    orders for disclosure 33
    patient requests for
        information. 105
    with diseases . . . 9-10, 89-90, 93-4
documents
    delivery up/destruction orders. . 66
    disclosure. 32, 33-4
    public interest
        immunity 35, 37-8, 39
DPA see Data Protection Act 1998
Driver and Vehicle Licensing
    Agency (DVLA) 89, 91-2
driving when unfit to do so . . 89, 91-2

Education Act 1996 . . . 126, 129, 130
education authorities 125-6
Education and Libraries (Northern
    Ireland) Order 1986 . . . . 127, 130
Education (Scotland) Act
    1980 . . . . 126, 127, 130
Ellis v Home Office [1953]. 36n
emergencies 86-7
employers 60, 87, 105
enforcement notices. 44-5
environmental issues. 106
equity
    account of profits. 65
    damages 67
    unconscionable behaviour 13
ethics committees 15-16, 89
European Commission. 53, 139
European Convention for the
    Protection of Human Rights
    and Fundamental
    Freedoms . . . 12, 40, 46-55, 57, 79

European Court of Human
   Rights 46, 49, 50, 51-3, 54, 55
European law
   Data Protection
      Directive 40, 41, 131, 139
   influence on Data Protection
      Act 1998 40-5
   influence on Human Rights
      Act 1998 46-55
exemplary damages 68-9

F v West Berkshire HA [1989] . . . 18-19
Family Law Reform Act
   1969 . . . . 16, 17, 18
fertility treatment 25-6
fiduciary responsibility 6, 66
financial loss 67
foreseeable distress 67, 68
Fraser v Evans [1969] 3n
freedom of expression 48, 54
Freedom of Information Bill . . 45, 59
freedom of thought, conscience
   and religion 48

Gartside v Outram [1856] 12n
GDC see General Dental Council
General Dental Council (GDC) . . 95-6
General Medical Council
   (GMC) . . 11-12, 14-16, 24, 61, 84-94
general practitioners see doctors
Gillick competence 18
Gillick v West Norfolk & Wisbech
   AHA [1985] 16, 17
GMC see General Medical Council
government servants 69
GPnet 43

Halcon International Ltd Inc v Shell
   Transport & Trading Co [1979] . . 33n
Handyside v UK [1976] 48n
Hayes v Dodd [1990] 67n
Health and Personal Social Services
   (Northern Ireland) Order 1972 . 128
Health and Personal Social Services
   (Northern Ireland) Order 1991 . 129
Health and Personal Social Services
   (Special Agencies) (Northern
      Ireland) Order 1990 128-9
health professionals

Chartered Society of
   Physiotherapists
      guidelines 102-6
   clinical relationship 7, 8
   data processing 140
   Data Protection Act 1998
      definition 44, 127-9
   disclosure within teams 86-7
   GDC guidelines 95-6
   GMC guidelines 84-94
   patients with communicable
      diseases 92-3
   patient's rights of access to
      health records 57, 58-9
   sensitive personal data
      processing 43
   with serious communicable
      diseases themselves 93-4
   UKCC guidelines 97-101
health records 27-8, 30, 31
   crime prevention 26
   Data Protection Act 1998 42
   dental 96
   European Court of
      Human Rights . . . 49-50, 51, 52
   Freedom of Information Bill . . 45
   public interest immunity 36
   research/teaching 101
   rights of access
      to 56-62, 88-9, 100-1
health visitors, UKCC
   guidelines 97-101
Hellewell v Chief Constable of Derbyshire
   [1995] 12
Heywood v Wellers [1976] 67n, 68
HIV 25, 50, 52, 93
Human Fertilisation and
   Embryology Act 1990 . . . . . 25, 26
Human Fertilisation and
   Embryology (Disclosure
   of Information) Act 1992 26
Human Rights Act 1998 . 23, 40, 46-55

implied obligation 1, 2, 7-8
infectious diseases 24-5
see also communicable diseases
iniquity cloaking 12-13
injunctions . . 9, 63-5, 70, 73, 76, 80-1
inspectors of taxes 90-1
insurance companies . . 60, 87, 88, 108
interim injunctions . 63-5, 73, 76, 80-1

Internet 43

Jarvis v Swan Tours Ltd [1973] . . . 67n
judicial investigation 90, 109

Kaye v Robertson [1991] 64n

Leigh v Gladstone [1909] 36n
Lennon v News Group Newspapers Ltd
 v Twist [1978] 5n
litigation 29-39
Lord Advocate v The Scotsman [1990] . 21

McGinley v UK [1999] 50n
Mahon v Rahn [1998] 34n
Malone v Metropolitan Police
 Commissioner [1979] 66-7
margin of appreciation 48-9
Medical Act 1983 128
medical emergencies 86-7
medical records *see* health records
medical reports 59-60
medical research 89, 101, 103
mental health 18-19, 26
Mental Health Act 1983 18
Mercer v St Helens & Knowsley Hospitals
 NHS Trust [1995] 37
midwives, UKCC guidelines . . 97-101
Ministers of the Crown Act 1975 . 129
Moore v Regents of the University of
 California [1990] 6n
Morrison v Moat [1851] 2
MS v Sweden [1999] 49-50, 51

National Health Service Act
 1977 . . . . 25n, 128
National Health Service and
 Community Care Act 1990 . . . 128
National Health Service (NHS)
 patient's rights of access to health
 records 57
 personal data 41, 45
 public interest immunity 37
National Health Service (Notification
 of Births and Deaths) Regulations
 1982 . . . . 25n
National Health Service (Scotland)
 Act 1978 128
National Health Service (Venereal
 Diseases) Regulations 1974 25
negligence 21, 22, 30

NHS *see* National Health Service
NHSnet 43
Nicholls v Rushton [1992] 67n
non-contractual breaches of
 confidence 66-7
non-disclosure
 Data Protection Act 1998 127
 negligent 21, 22
 public interest . . . 9, 11, 14, 36, 38
non-parties 33
Norwich Pharmacal Co v Customs and
 Excise Commissioners [1974] 70
Norwich Pharmacal orders . . . 69-70
nurses, UKCC guidelines . . . 97-101

occupational health doctors 60
official requests for information . . 105
Official Secrets Act 1989 21
Opticians Act 1989 127
orders
 delivery up/destruction 66
 disclosure 33, 34, 90
 Norwich Pharmacal 69-70
Osteopaths Act 1993 128

Palmer v Tees HA [1908] 22n
patients
 access to health records after
  death 61, 88-9
 Chartered Society of
  Physiotherapists
  guidelines 102-5
 children 16-18
 disclosure in medical interests . 87-8
 disclosure upon death . . 3, 15, 88-9
 driving when unfit to do
  so 89, 91-2
 GMC guidelines 84-5, 86-9
 mental disorder 18-19
 need for confidentiality 1
 right of access to health
  records 56-62
 serious communicable
  diseases 92-3
 UKCC guidelines 98
Patient's Charter 56
peace of mind 67, 68
penalties 23
permanent injunctions . . . 65, 73, 80
personal data . 41-2, 43-5, 58, 111, 112
 automated decision-taking . . 121-3

compensation 123-5
data protection principles . . 131-7
exemptions 125-7
prevention of processing likely to
  cause damage or distress . 119-20
prevention of processing for
  purposes of direct
  marketing 121
recipient definition 130
rights of access 44, 115-19
see also sensitive personal data
personal injury 30, 49-50, 51
personal records 26
Peter Pan Manufacturing Corporation
  v Corsets Silhouette Ltd [1964] . . . 65n
Pharmacy Act 1954 127
Pharmacy (Northern Ireland)
  Order 1976 127
Phipps v Boardman [1967] 66n
Police and Criminal Evidence Act
  1984 (PACE 1984) 26
pre-action protocols 30-1
precedents 71-83
Prevention of Terrorism (Temporary
  Provisions) Act 1989 27
Price Waterhouse v BCCI Holdings
  (Luxembourg) SA [1992] 69n
Prince Albert v Strange [1849] 66n
prisoners 36
privacy 49-50
private hospitals 37-8
Professions Supplementary to
  Medicine Act 1960 128
profits
  account of 65
  exceeding compensation payable
    to claimant 69
  injunctions unable to prevent . . 64
proportionality doctrine 48
public authorities, Human Rights
  Act 1998 47
Public Health (Control of Disease)
  Act 1984 24
Public Health (Infectious Diseases)
  Regulations 1998 24-5
public interest 3, 8-12, 13, 14, 52
  case study 75, 77, 82
  Data Protection Act 1998 140
  detriment 19-20
  GDC guidelines 95
  GMC guidelines 89-90

immunity 34-9
UKCC guidelines 98-9

R v Chief Constable of West Midlands,
  ex parte Wiley [1994] 34-5
R v Department of Health ex parte Source
  Informatics Ltd [2000] 6, 13
R v K [1993] 36
R v Mid Glamorgan Family Health
  Services, ex parte Martin
  [1995] 54n, 56n, 57-8
R v North & East Devon HA,
  ex parte Coughlan [1999] 54n
R v Secretary of State for the Home
  Department, ex parte Benson
  [1988] 36
R v Secretary of State for the Home
  Department, ex parte Duggan
  [1994] 36n
R v SoS for Home Department,
  ex parte Tremayne 54n
racial origin 43-4, 140
Re Cable [1975] 64n
Re L (Patient: Non-consensual
  Treatment) [1997] 19
Re N [1999] 22n
Re R (a Minor) (Wardship: Medical
  Treatment) [1991] 17n
relevant filing system 111, 112
remedies 5, 21, 47, 63-70
requests for
  information 104-6, 116-19
research 15, 89, 101, 103
rights
  access to health
    records 56-62, 88-9, 100-1
  access to personal data . 44, 115-19
  data processing   119-21, 138,
                            139, 140-1

  Data Protection Act
    exemptions 127
  data subjects 115-25
  Human Rights Act 1998 . . . 46-55
  prevention of data processing
    likely to cause damage or
    distress 44, 119-20
  prevention of data processing
    for purposes of direct
    marketing 44, 121
  in relation to automated
    decision-taking 44, 121-3

Road Traffic Act 1988 27
Robb v Green [1895]. 66n
Rookes v Barnard [1964] 68-9
Royal College of Veterinary
    Surgeons 107-9

*Saltman Engineering Co v Campbell
    Engineering Co Ltd* [1948] . . . 4, 66n
Schering Chemicals Ltd v Falkman Ltd
    [1981] 10
schools 125, 126-7, 129-30
Self-Governing Schools etc (Scotland)
    Act 1989 126
sensitive personal
    data . . . 41, 42, 43, 79, 112, 138-41
sexually transmitted diseases 25
Sheffield v UK [1999] 50n
Smith v ILEA [1978] 64n
social work 126
'special purposes'. 113
Spycatcher case [1990]. 65n
status quo ante, interim injunctions. 64
statute 3, 23-8, 69
Stephens v Avery [1988] 4n, 7
suing 3-4, 99
Supreme Court Act 1981 . 30n, 33, 66
Supreme Court of Finland 50
*Sutherland Publishing Co Ltd v Caxton
    Publishing Co Ltd* [1936] 65n

tax inspectors 90-1
*Taylor v Director of the Serious Fraud
    Office* [1999] 34n
teaching 89, 101
teams, disclosure within . . . 86-7, 104

Times Newspapers Ltd v MGN Ltd
    [1993] 65n
tort, damages 67
transsexuals 50
trusts, constructive 66
Tyrer v UK [1978] 48n

UKCC *see* United Kingdom Central
    Council for Nursing, Midwifery
    and Health Visiting
unconscionable
    behaviour 3, 6, 7, 8, 13-14, 68
United Kingdom Central Council for
    Nursing, Midwifery and Health
    Visiting (UKCC) 97-101
*United Scientific Holdings Ltd v Burnley
    Borough Council* [1978]. 67n
Universal Thermosensor Ltd v Hibben
    [1992] 65n

*W (A Minor) (Medical Treatment: Court's
    Jurisdiction)* [1992] 17-18
W v Egdell [1990]. 3n, 10-12, 14, 75, 77
Wednesbury unreasonableness
    doctrine 49
Williams v Settle [1960] 69n
Williams v Star Newspaper Co Ltd
    [1908] 36n
witnesses 27-8
Woodward v Hutchins [1977] 5n

X v Y and others [1988] . . 9-10, 25n, 77

Z v Finland [1998] . . . 49n, 50n, 52-3